Y0-BRN-795

THE
Best English and
Scottish Ballads

SELECTED BY

EDWARD A. BRYANT

"Certainly, I must confesse my owne baibarousnes, I neuer heard the olde song of PERCY *and* DUGLAS *that I found not my heart mooued more then with a Trumpet."*
—SIR PHILIP SIDNEY.

Granger Poetry Library

GRANGER BOOK CO., INC.
Great Neck, N.Y.

First Published 1911

Reprinted 1982

LC 81-84877
ISBN 0-89609-228-3

Printed in the U.S.A.

TO

THE MEMORY OF

FRANCIS JAMES CHILD

THIS BOOK OF BALLADS

IS DEDICATED

PREFACE

THE ballads comprising the following collection
are those English and Scottish tales of olden time
which had their origin among the common people
and were a feature of primitive community life.
They have been chosen from collections made by
scholars of the eighteenth and nineteenth centuries,
one of the most notable of whom was Bishop Thomas
Percy, whose "Reliques of Ancient Poetry" was
published in 1765. Sir Walter Scott, an enthusiastic
student of the "Reliques," carried on the pursuit of
ballad-collecting by first-hand researches among the
people of the Border. In 1802 and 1803 were published six volumes of ballads and folk-songs of his
own collecting, under the title, "Minstrelsy of the
Scottish Border." More recent devotees of the
subject were Francis James Child, who was still
engaged in his work of collecting, collating, and
sifting his material at the time of his death in 1896,
and his co-workers in this field, Frederick J. Furnivall (died in 1910) and John W. Hales.

The scope of the present collection is indicated by
the title. In comparatively brief space are here
included the best of the great old ballads, and at the
same time those best suited to illustrate the various

types of this style of lyric. The order of arrangement adopted is a quite arbitrary one. These tales
in verse are of course both anonymous and undated,
preventing their listing by authors or chronologi-
cally. The plan decided on has been to place in
Book I ballads dealing with magic and the super-
natural; in Book II, tales of pure romance, such
as "Childe Maurice," "Lord Ingram," and "Fair
Margaret"; in Book III, tales of romance shading
off into real history, as "Sir Patrick Spens," "Hugh
of Lincoln," and "The Bonny Earl of Murray";
in Book IV, the Robin Hood ballads; in Book V,
ballads dealing chiefly with historical topics, from
"Durham Field," "Otterburn," and "Chevy
Chase," down to less-renowned Border feuds; and
in Book VI, certain late ballads, among them some
of the best-known,— e.g. "Barbara Allen". and
"Lord Bateman,"— but revealing this form of verse
at once at the height of perfection and at the begin-
ning of its decline. In this arrangement the work
follows to an extent the idea of Sir A. T. Quiller-
Couch in his admirable "Oxford" collection,— in
which, it may be added, that experienced author and
anthologizer renders the same service to the ballad
as to all literary subjects which he touches.

It is to be regretted that in carrying out the idea
of producing a compact volume it was possible to
include only three of the set of ballads celebrating

the deeds of "Robin Hood and his meiny,"—ballads which have formed the basis of many complete books devoted to the adventures of these dwellers in the good greenwood. The three selected are typical of their class.

The text followed is in general that of the Percy Folio MS., edited by Professors Hales and Furnivall. A few changes in the way of omissions of too broad verses and toning down of coarse phrases, with due care not to change the sense, have been made. As Quiller-Couch says, in the Introduction to his edition, "It seems wiser to omit a stanza from 'Glasgerion,' for example, or to modify a line in 'Young Hunting,' than to withhold these beautiful things altogether from boy or maid."

For valuable information on the subject of ballad literature the editor is under obligations also to Allingham's Preface to his "Ballad Book" and Miss Adelaide Witham's Introduction to "English and Scottish Popular Ballads." Of chief assistance has been the vast fund of information contained in Professor Child's exhaustive work, to which every present-day student of the ballad is bound to pay grateful tribute. If the interest of readers of this collection is stimulated to more extended investigation of the subject as discussed in Professor Childs' volumes, any efforts put forth in its preparation will have been repaid.   E. A. B.

CONTENTS

BOOK I

BOOK II

BOOK III

BOOK IV

BOOK V

BOOK VI

" 'What is a ballad?'—'A ballad is *The Mill-dams of Binnorie* and *Sir Patrick Spens* and *The Duglas Tragedy* and *Lord Randal* and *Childe Maurice,* and things of that sort.' "

—W. P. KER, *On the History of Ballads.*

BOOK I

THOMAS THE RHYMER

1. TRUE Thomas lay on Huntlie bank;
      A ferlie he spied wi' his e'e;
   And there he saw a ladye bright
      Come riding down by the Eildon Tree

2. Her skirt was o' the grass-green silk,
      Her mantle o' the velvet fyne;
   At ilka tett o' her horse's mane
      Hung fifty siller bells and nine.

3. True Thomas he pu'd aff his cap,
      And louted low down on his knee:
   'Hail to thee, Mary, Queen of Heaven
      For thy peer on earth could never be.'

4. 'O no, O no, Thomas,' she said,
      'That name does not belang to me;
   I'm but the Queen o' fair Elfland,
      That am hither come to visit thee.

5. 'Harp and carp, Thomas,' she said;
      'Harp and carp along wi' me;
   And if ye dare to kiss my lips,
      Sure of your bodie I will be.'

6. 'Betide me weal, betide me woe,
      That weird shall never daunten me.'
   Syne he has kiss'd her rosy lips,
      All underneath the Eildon Tree.

7. 'Now ye maun go wi' me,' she said,
      'True Thomas, ye maun go wi' me;
   And ye maun serve me seven years,
      Thro' weal or woe as may chance to be.'

8. She's mounted on her milk-white steed,
      She's ta'en true Thomas up behind;
   And aye, whene'er her bridle rang,
      The steed gaed swifter than the wind.

9. O they rade on, and farther on,
      The steed gaed swifter than the wind;
   Until they reach'd a desert wide,
      And living land was left behind.

10. 'Light down, light down now, true Thomas,
      And lean your head upon my knee;
   Abide ye there a little space,
      And I will show you ferlies three.

11. 'O see ye not yon narrow road,
      So thick beset wi' thorns and briers?
   That is the Path of Righteousness,
      Though after it but few inquires.

12. 'And see ye not yon braid, braid road,
    That lies across the lily leven?
    That is the Path of Wickedness,
    Though some call it the Road to Heaven.

13. 'And see ye not yon bonny road
    That winds about the fernie brae?
    That is the Road to fair Elfland,
    Where thou and I this night maun gae.

14. 'But, Thomas, ye sall haud your tongue,
    Whatever ye may hear or see;
    For speak ye word in Elflyn-land,
    Ye'll ne'er win back to your ain countrie.'

15. O they rade on, and farther on,
    And they waded rivers abune the knee
    And they saw neither sun nor moon,
    But they heard the roaring of the sea.

16. It was mirk, mirk night, there was nae starlight,
    They waded thro' red blude to the knee;
    For a' the blude that's shed on the earth
    Rins through the springs o' that countrie

17. Syne they came to a garden green,
    And she pu'd an apple frae a tree:
    'Take this for thy wages, true Thomas;
    It will give thee the tongue that can never lee.'

18. 'My tongue is my ain,' true Thomas he said
    'A gudely gift ye wad gie to me!
I neither dought to buy or sell
    At fair or tryst where I might be.

19. 'I dought neither speak to prince or peer,
    Nor ask of grace from fair ladye!'—
'Now haud thy peace, Thomas,' she said,
    'For as I say, so must it be.'

20. He has gotten a coat of the even cloth,
    And a pair o' shoon of the velvet green:
And till seven years were gane and past,
    True Thomas on earth was never seen

SIR CAWLINE

1. *JESUS, Lord mickle of might,*
    That dyed for us on roode,
So maintaine us in all our right
    That loves true English blood!

2. Sir Cawline was an English knight
    Curteous and full hardye;
And our King has lent him forth to fight,
    Into Ireland over the sea.

3. And in that land there dwells a King,
    Over all the bell does beare;

.   And he hath a ladye to his daughter,
    Of fashion she hath no peere;
Knights and lordes they woo'd her both,
    Trusted to have been her feere.

4. Sir Cawline loves her best of onie,
    But nothing durst he say
To discreeve his councell to no man,
    But dearlye loved this may.

5. Till it befell upon a day,
    Great dill to him was dight;
The mayden's love removed his mind,
    To care-bed went the knight.

6. One while he spread his armes him fro,
    And cryed so pittyouslye:
'For the mayden's love that I have most
       minde
    This day shall comfort mee,
Or else ere noone I shall be dead!'
    Thus can Sir Cawline say.

7. When the parish mass that itt was done,
    And the King was bowne to dine,
Says, 'Where is Sir Cawline, that was wont
    To serve me with ale and wine?'

8. But then answer'd a curteous knight
    Fast his hands wringinge:

'Sir Cawline's sicke and like to be dead　.
　Without and a good leechìnge.'

9. 'Feitch ye downe my daughter deere,
　　She is a leeche full fine;
　　Ay, and take you doe and the baken bread,
　　And drinke he of the wine soe red,
　　And looke no daynty's for him too deare,
　　For full loth I wo'ld him tine.'

10. This ladye is gone to his chamber,
　　Her maydens following nye;
　　'O well,' she saith, 'how doth my lord?'
　　'O sicke!' againe saith hee.

11. 'But rise up wightlye, man, for shame!
　　Ne'er lie here soe cowardlye!
　　Itt is told in my father's hall
　　For my love you will dye.'—

12. 'Itt is for your love, fayre ladye,
　　That all this dill I drie;
　　For if you wo'ld comfort me with a kisse,
　　Then were I brought from bale to bliss,
　　No longer here wo'ld I lye.'—

13. 'Alas! soe well you know, Sir Knight,
　　I cannot be your feere.'—
　　'Yet some deeds of armes fain wo'ld I doe
　　To be your bacheleere.'—

14. 'On Eldritch Hill there grows a tnorn,
    Upon the mores brodinge;
  And wo'ld you, Sir Knight, wake there all
        night
    To day of the other morninge?

15. 'For the Eldritch King, that is mickle of
        might,
    Will examine you beforne:
  There was never a man bare his life away
    Since the day that I was born.'—

16. 'But I will for your sake, ladye,
    Walk on the bents soe browne,
  And I'll either bring you a readye token,
    Or I'll ne'er come to you again.'

17. But this ladye is gone to her chamber,
    Her maydens following bright;
  And Sir Cawline's gone to the mores soe
        broad,
    For to wake there all night.

18. Unto midnight that the moone did rise
    He walkèd up and downe,
  And a lightsome bugle then heard he blow
    Over the bents so browne;
  Sayes he, 'And if cryance come to my heart,
    I am farr from any good towne.'

19. And he spyèd, e'en a little him by,
      A furyous king and a fell,
    And a ladye bright his brydle led
      More seemlye than onie can tell.

20. Soe fast he call'd on Sir Cawline,
      'O man, I rede thee flye!
    For if cryance come until thy heart
      I'm afeard lest thou maun dye!'—

21. He sayes, 'No cryance comes to my heart,
      Nor i' faith I fear not thee;
    For because thou ming'd not Christ before,
      The lesse me dreadeth thee.'

22. But Sir Cawline then he shooke a speare;
      The King was bold, ánd abode:
    And the timber those two children bare
      Soe soon in sunder slode:
    Forth they tooke and two good swords,
      And they layden on good loade.

23. The Eldritch King was mickle of might,
      And stiffly to the ground did stand;
    But Sir Cawline with an aukeward stroke
      He brought from him his hand —
    Ay, and flying over his head so hye
      It fell down of that lay land.

24. His ladye stood a little thereby,
      Fast her hands wringìnge:

'For the mayden's love that you have most
    minde,
  Smyte you noe more this King.

25. 'And he's never come upon Eldritch Hill
    Him to sport, gammon or play,
  And to meet no man of middle-earth
    That lives on Christ his lay.'

26. But he then up, that Eldritch King,
    Set him in his sadle againe,
  And that Eldritch King and his ladye
    To their castle are they gone.

27. Sir Cawline took up that eldritch sword
    As hard as any flynt,
  Soe did he the hand with ringès five
    Harder than fyer, and brent.

28. The watchmen cryed upon the walls
    And sayd, 'Sir Cawline's slaine!'
  Then the King's daughter she fell downe
    'For peerlesse is my payne!'—

29. 'O peace, my ladye!' sayes Sir Cawline,
    'I have bought thy love full deare;
  O peace, my ladye!' sayes Sir Cawline,
    'Peace, ladye, for I am heere!'

30. He's presented to the King's daughter
    The hand, and then the sword;

And he has claimed the King's daughter
According to her word.

31. And the King has betaken him his broad lands
And all his venison;
Sayes, 'Thou shalt have my daughter deare,
And be my onelye son.'

WILLY'S LADY

1. SWEET Willy's ta'en him o'er the faem,
He's woo'd a wife and brought her hame.

2. He's woo'd her for her yellow hair,
But his mither wrought her mickle care;

3. And mickle dolour gar'd her drie,
For lighter she can never be.

4. But in her bower she sits wi' pain,
And Willy mourns o'er her in vain.

5. And to his mither he has gane;
That vile rank witch of vilest kind.

6. He says: 'My ladie has a cup
Wi' gowd and silver set about.

7. 'This goodlie gift shall be your ain,
And let her be lighter o' her young bairn.' —

8. 'Of her young bairn she'll ne'er be lighter,
   Nor in her bower to shine the brighter:

9. 'But she shall die and turn to clay,
   And you shall wed another may.'—

10. 'Another may I'll marry nane,
    Another may I'll ne'er bring hame.'

11. But sighing says his bonnie wife,
    'I wish this was an end o' my life!

12. 'Yet gae ye unto your mither again,
    That vile rank witch of vilest kind.

13. 'And say: My ladie has a steed,
    The like o' him's no in the lands of Leed.

14. 'For at ilka tett o' that horse's mane
    There's a golden chess and a bell ringing.

15. 'This goodlie gift shall be your ain,
    And let her be lighter o' her young bairn.' —

16. 'O' her young bairn she'll ne'er be lighter,
    Nor in her bower to shine the brighter;

17. 'But she shall die and turn to clay,
    And ye shall wed another may.'—

18. 'Another may I'll marry nane,
    Another may I'll ne'er bring hame.'

19. But sighing says his bonnie wife,
    'I wish this was an end o' my life!

20. 'Yet gae ye unto your mither again,
    That vile rank witch of vilest kind:

21. 'And say: My ladie has a girdle,
    It's a' red gowd unto the middle.

22. 'And ay at every silver hem
    Hangs fifty silver bells and ten.

23. 'That goodlie gift shall be your ain,
    But let her be lighter o' her young bairn.'—

24. 'O' her young bairn she's ne'er be lighter,
    Nor in her bower to shine the brighter:

25. 'But she shall die and turn to clay,
    And you shall wed another may.'—

26. 'Another may I'll never wed nane,
    Another may I'll never bring hame.'

27. But sighing says his bonnie wife,
    'I wish this was an end o' my life!'

28. Then out and spake the Billy Blind —
    He spake aye in a good time;

29. 'Ye doe ye to the market-place,
    And there buy ye a loaf o' wax;

30. 'Ye shape it bairn and bairnly like,
    And in twa glasses e'en ye'll pit.

31. 'And do ye to your mither then,
    And bid her come to your boy's christ'nen,

32. 'For dear's the boy he's been to you:
    Then notice weel what she shall do:

33. 'And do you stand a little away,
    And listen weel what she shall say.'

34. He did him to the market-place,
    And there he bought a loaf o' wax.

35. He shaped it bairn and bairnly-like,
    And in 't twa glasses e'en he pat.

36. He did him till his mither then,
    And bade her to his boy's christ'nen.

37. And he did stand a little forbye,
    And noticed well what she did say.

38. 'O wha has loosed the nine witch-knots
    That was among that ladie's locks?

39. 'And wha has ta'en out the kaims o' care
    That hangs among that ladie's hair?

40. 'And wha's ta'en down the bush o' woodbine
    That hangs atween her bower and mine?

41. 'And wha has kill'd the master kid
    That ran aneath that ladie's bed?

42. 'And wha has loosed her left-foot shee
    And letten that ladie lighter be?'

43. Syne Willy has loosed the nine witch-knots
    That was among his ladie's locks:

44. And Willy's ta'en out the kaims o' care
    That hang among his ladie's hair:

45. And Willy's ta'en down the bush o' woodbine
    That hang atween her bower and thine:

46. And Willy has kill'd the master kid
    That ran aneath his ladie's bed:

47. And Willy has loosed her left-foot shee,
    And letten his ladie lighter be.

48. And now he's gotten a bonny young son,
    And mickle grace be him upon!

THE QUEEN OF ELFLAND'S NOURICE

1. '*I HEARD a cow low, a bonnie cow low,*
    And a cow low down in yon glen:
    Lang, lang will my young son greet
    Or his mither bid him come ben!

2. '*I heard a cow low, a bonnie cow low,*
    And a cow low down in yon fauld:
   Lang, lang will my young son greet
    Or his mither take him frae cauld!'

3. The Queen of Elfland's nourice
    She sits and sings her lane
   'Waken, Queen of Elfland,
   And hear your nourice moan.'—

4. 'O moan ye for your meat,
    Or moan ye for your fee,
   Or moan ye for the ither bounties
    That ladies are wont to gie?'—

5. 'I moan na for my meat,
    Nor moan I for my fee,
   Nor moan I for the ither bounties
    That ladies are wont to gie.

6. 'But I heard a bonnie cow
    Low down in yonder fauld
   And I moan for my young son
    I left in four nights auld.

7. 'I moan na for my meat,
    Nor yet for my fee;
   But I moan for Christen land;
    It's there I fain would be.'

8. 'O nurse my bairn, nourice,
    Till he stan' at your knee,
  An ye's win hame to Christen land
    Whar fain it's ye wad be.

9. 'O keep my bairn, nourice,
    Till he gang by the hauld,
  An ye's win hame to your young son
    Ye left in four nights auld.

10. 'O nourice lay your head
     Here upo' my knee:
   See ye not that narrow road
     Up by yonder tree?

11. 'See ye not the narrow road
     By yon lillie leven?
   That's the road the righteous goes
     And that's the road to heaven.

12. 'An' see na ye that braid road
     Down by yon sunny fell?
   Yon's the road the wicked gae,
     An' that's the road to hell.

13. An' see na ye that bonny road
     About the fernie brae?
   That wins back frae Elfland
     Where you must wait to gae.

LADY ISABEL AND THE ELF-KNIGHT

1. *MY plaid awa', my plaid awa',*
   And o'er the hill and far awa';
   And far awa' to Norrowa',
   My plaid shall not be blown awa'!

2. Lady Isabel sits in her bower sewing,
   Aye as the gowans grow gay —
   She heard an elf-knight his horn blawing,
   The first morning in May.

3. The elf-knight sits on yon hill,
   He blaws his horn baith loud and shrill.

4. He blaws it east, he blaws it west,
   He blaws it where he lyketh best.

5. 'I wish that horn were in my kist,
   Yea, and the knight in my arms niest.'

6. She had no sooner these words said,
   When that knight came to her bed.

7. 'Thou art owre young a maid,' quoth he,
   'Married with me thou ill wouldst be.'—

8. 'I have a sister younger than I,
   And she was married yesterday.'—

9. 'Married with me if thou wouldst be,
   A courtesie thou must do to me.

10. 'For thou must shape a sark to me
    Without any cut or hem,' quoth he:

11. 'It's ye maun shape it knife-and-shurlesse,
    And also sew it needle-threedlesse.

12. 'And ye maun wash it in yonder well,
    Where the dew never wat nor the rain never
      fell.

13. 'And ye maun dry it upon a thorn
    That never budded sin Adam was born.'—

14. 'Now sin ye have asked some things o' me,
    It's right I ask as mony o' thee.

15. 'My father he ask'd me an acre o' land
    Between the saut sea and the strand.

16. 'And ye maun are it wi' your blawin' horn,
    And ye maun sow it wi' pepper corn.

17. 'And ye maun harrow it with ae tyne,
    And ye maun shear it with ae horse bane.

18. 'And ye maun stack it in yon mouse-hole,
    And ye maun thresh it in yon shoe-sole.

19. 'And ye maun winnow it in your loof,
    And ye maun sack it in your glove.

20. 'And ye maun bring it owre the sea,
    Fair and clean and dry to me.

21. 'And when ye've done an' finish'd your wark,
Come to me, love, an' get your sark.'

22. 'It's I'll not quit my plaid for my life;
It haps my seven bairns and my wife.'
The wind sall not blow my plaid awa':
'And it's I will keep me a maiden still,
Let the elfin knight do what he will'—
The wind has not blawn my plaid awa'!

MAY COLVIN

1. FALSE Sir John a-wooing came
To a maid of beauty fair;
May Colvin was this lady's name,
Her father's only heir.

2. He woo'd her but, he woo'd her ben,
He woo'd her in the ha';
Until he got the lady's consent
To mount and ride awa'.

3. 'Go fetch me some of your father's gold,
And some of your mother's fee,
And I'll carry you into the north land,
And there I'll marry thee.'

4. She's gane to her father's coffers
Where all his money lay,

And she's taken the red, and she's left the
    white,
    And so lightly she's tripp'd away.

5. She's gane to her father's stable
    Where all the steeds did stand,
  And she's taken the best, and she's left the
    warst
    That was in her father's land.

6. She's mounted on a milk-white steed,
    And he on a dapple-grey,
  And on they rade to a lonesome part,
    A rock beside the sea.

7. 'Loup off the steed,' says false Sir John,
    'Your bridal bed you see;
  Seven ladies I have drownèd here,
    And the eight' one you shall be.

8. 'Cast off, cast off your silks so fine
    And lay them on a stone,
  For they are too fine and costly
    To rot in the salt sea foam.

9. 'Cast off, cast off your silken stays,
    For and your broider'd shoon,
  For they are too fine and costly
    To rot in the salt sea foam.

10. 'Cast off, cast off your Holland smock
  That's border'd with the lawn,
 For it is too fine and costly
  To rot in the salt sea foam.'—

11. 'O turn about, thou false Sir John,
  And look to the leaf o' the tree;
 For it never became a gentleman
  A naked woman to see.'

12. He turn'd himself straight round about
  To look to the leaf o' the tree;
 She's twined her arms about his waist
  And thrown him into the sea.

13. 'O hold a grip o' me, May Colvin,
  For fear that I should drown;
 I'll take you home to your father's bower
  And safe I'll set you down.'

14. 'No help, no help, thou false Sir John,
  No help, no pity thee!
 For you lie not in a caulder bed
  Than you thought to lay me.'

15. She mounted on her milk-white steed,
  And led the dapple-grey,
 And she rode till she reach'd her father's
   gate,
  At the breakin' o' the day.

16. Up then spake the pretty parrot,
      'May Colvin, where have you been?
    What has become o' false Sir John ·
      That went with you yestreen?'—

17. 'O hold your tongue, my pretty parrot!
      Nor tell no tales o' me;
    Your cage shall be made o' the beaten gold
      And the spokes o' ivorie.'

18. Up then spake her father dear,
      In the bed-chamber where he lay:
    'What ails the pretty parrot,
      That prattles so long ere day?'—

19. 'There came a cat to my cage, master,
      I thought 't would have worried me,
    And I was calling to May Colvin
      To take the cat from me.'

THE WEE WEE MAN

1. As I was walking mine alane
     Atween a water and a wa',
   There I spied a wee wee man,
     And he was the least that ere I saw.

2. His legs were scant a shathmont's length,
     And thick and thimber was his thie;

Atween his brows there was a span,
  And atween his shoulders there was three.

3. He's ta'en and flung a meikle stane,
    And he flang 't as far as I could see;
   Though I had been a Wallace wight
    I couldna liften 't to my knee.

4. 'O wee wee man, but ye be strang!
    O tell me where your dwelling be?'
   'My dwelling's down by yon bonny bower;
    Fair lady, come wi' me and see.'

5. On we lap, and awa' we rade,
    Till we came to yon bonny green;
   We lighted down to bait our steed,
    And out there came a lady sheen;

6. Wi' four and twenty at her back
    A' comely clad in glisterin' green;
   Tho' the King of Scotland had been there,
    The warst o' them might ha' been his
      queen.

7. On we lap, and awa' we rade,
    Till we came to a bonny ha';
   The roof was o' the beaten gowd,
    And the floor was o' the cristal a'.

8. When we came to the stair-foot,
    Ladies were dancing jimp and sma',

But in the twinkling of an eie
My wee wee man was clean awa'.

9. Out gat the lights, on came the mist,
    Ladies nor mannie mair cou'd I see·
I turn'd about, and gae a look
    Just at the foot o' Benachie.

ALISON GROSS

1. O ALISON GROSS, that lives in yon tow'r,
    The ugliest witch i' the north countrie,
Has trysted me ae day up till her bow'r
    And mony fair speeches she made to me.

2. She straik'd my head an' she kaim'd my hair,
    And she set me down saftly on her knee;
Says, 'Gin ye will be my lemman sae true,
    Sae mony braw things as I would you gie!

3. She show'd me a mantle o' red scarlét,
    Wi' gouden flowers an' fringes fine;
Says, 'Gin ye will be my lemman sae true,
    This gudely gift it sall be thine.'—

4. 'Awa', awa', ye ugly witch,
    Haud far awa', an' lat me be!
I never will be your lemman sae true,
    An' I wish I were out o' your company.'

5. She neist brought a sark o' the saftest silk,
    Well wrought wi' pearls about the band;
    Says, 'Gin ye will be my lemman sae true,
      This gudely gift ye sall command.'

6. She show'd me a cup o' the good red gowd,
    Well set wi' jewels sae fair to see;
    Says, 'Gin ye will be my lemman sae true,
      This gudely gift I will you gie.'—

7. 'Awa', awa', ye ugly witch,
    Haud far awa', an' lat me be!
    For I wouldna once kiss your ugly mouth
      For a' the gifts that ye could gie.'

8. She's turn'd her right an' roun' about,
    An' thrice she blaw on a grass-green horn;
    An' she sware by the moon an' the stars abune
      That she'd gar me rue the day I was born.

9. Then out has she ta'en a silver wand,
    An' she's turn'd her three times roun' and
      roun';
  She mutter'd sic words till my strength it fail'd,
    An' I fell down senseless upon the groun'.

10. She's turn'd me into an ugly worm,
    And gar'd me toddle about the tree;
    An' ay, on ilka Saturday's night,
      My sister Maisry came to me,

11. Wi' silver bason an' silver kaim
    To kaim my headie upon her knee;
    But or I had kiss'd wi' Alison Gross
    I'd sooner ha' toddled about the tree.

12. But as it fell out, on last Hallowe'en,
    When the Seely Court was ridin' by,
    The Queen lighted down on a gowany bank
    Nae far frae the tree where I wont to lye.

13. She took me up in her milk-white han',
    An' she 's straik'd me three times o'er her
        knee;
    She changed me again to my ain proper shape,
    An' nae mair I toddle about the tree.

KEMP OWYNE

1. HER mother died when she was young,
    Which gave her cause to make great moan;
    Her father married the warst woman
    That ever lived in Christendom.

2. She servèd her wi' foot and hand
    In everything that she could dee,
    Till once, in an unlucky time,
    She threw her owre a craig o' the sea.

3. Says, 'Lie you there, dove Isabel,
    And all my sorrows lie wi' thee!

Till Kemp Owyne come to the craig,
    And borrow you wi' kisses three.'

4. Her breath grew strang, her hair grew lang
    And twisted thrice about the tree,
    And all the people, far and near,
    Thought that a savage beast was she.

5. And aye she cried for Kemp Owyne
    Gin that he would but com' to her hand:—
    Now word has gane to Kemp Owyne
    That siccan a beast was in his land.

6. 'Now by my sooth,' says Kemp Owyne,
    'This fiery beast I'll gang to see';
    'And by my sooth,' says Segramour,
    'My ae brother, I'll gang you wi'.'

7. O they have biggit a bonny boat,
    And they have set her to the sea;
    But a mile before they reach'd the shore
    I wot she gar'd the red fire flee.

8. 'O brother, keep my boat afloat,
    An' lat her na the land so near!
    For the wicked beast she'll sure go mad,
    An' set fire to the land an' mair.'

9. Syne he has bent an arblast bow
    And aim'd an arrow at her head,

And swore, if she didna quit the land,
    Wi' that same shaft to shoot her dead.

10. 'O out o' my stythe I winna rise —
     And it is na for the fear o' thee —
    Till Kemp Owyne, the king's son,
      Come to the craig an' thrice kiss me.'

11. Her breath was strang, her hair was lang
     And twisted thrice about the tree,
    And with a swing she came about:
      'Come to the craig, an' kiss with me!

12. 'Here is a royal belt,' she cried,
     'That I have found in the green sea;
    And while your body it is on,
      Drawn shall your blood never be;
    But if you touch me, tail or fin,
      I swear my belt your death shall be.'

13. He's louted him o'er the Eastmuir craig,
     As out she swang and about the tree;
    He steppèd in, gave her a kiss,
      The royal belt he brought him wi'.

14. Her breath was strang, her hair was lang
     And twisted twice about the tree,
    As awa' she gid, and again she swang —
      'Come to the craig, an' kiss with me!

15. 'Here is a royal ring,' she said,
        'That I have found in the green sea;
    And while your finger it is on,
        Drawn shall your blood never be;
    But if you touch me, tail or fin,
        I swear my ring your death shall be.'

16. He's louted him o'er the Eastmuir craig,
        As out she swang and about the tree;
    He stepped in, gave her a kiss,
        The royal ring he brought him wi'.

17. Her breath was strang, her hair was lang
        And twisted ance about the tree,
    As awa' she gid and again she swang —
        'Come to the craig, an' kiss with me!

18. 'Here is a royal brand,' she said,
        'That I have found in the green sea;
    And while your body it is on,
        Drawn shall your blood never be;
    But if you touch me, tail or fin,
        I swear my brand your death shall be.'

19. He's louted him o'er the Eastmuir craig,
        As out she swang and about the tree;
    He steppèd in, gave her a kiss
        That royal brand he brought him wi'.

20. Her breath was sweet, her hair grew short,
        And twisted nane about the tree,

As awa' she gid and again she came
The fairest lady that ever could be.

21. 'O was it a wer-wolf into the wood,
Or was it a mermaid into the sea,
Or was it a man or a vile woman,
My true love, that mis-shapit thee?'—

22. 'It was na wer-wolf into the wood,
Nor was it mermaid into the sea,
But and it was my vile stepmother,
And wae and weary mote she be!

23. 'O a heavier weird shall light her on,
Her hair sall grow rough an' her teeth grow
lang,
And aye on her four feet sall she gang,
And aye in Wormeswood sall she won!'

BONNIE ANNIE

1. THERE was a rich lord, and he lived in Forfar,
He had a fair lady and one only dochter.

2. O she was fair! O dear, she was bonnie!
A ship's captain courted her to be his honey.

3. 'Ye'll steal your father's gowd, and your
mother's money,
And I'll make ye a lady in Ireland bonnie.'

4. She's stown her father's gowd, and her mother's
        money,
    But she was never a lady in Ireland bon:.ie.

5. They hadna sail'd far till the young thing cried
        'Woman!'
    'What can a woman do, lov., I will do for ye.

6. 'Lay about, steer about, lay our ship cannie,
    Do all ye can to save my dear Annie.'

7. 'There's fey folk in our ship, she winna sail for
        me,
    There's fey folk in our ship, she winna sail ony.'

8. They've castin' black bullets twice six and forty,
    And ae the black bullet fell on bonnie Annie.

9. 'Ye'll tak me in your arms twa, lo, lift me cannie,
    Throw me out owre-board, your ain dear Annie.'

10. He has ta'en her in his arms twa, lo, lifted her
        cannie,
    He has laid her on a bed of down, his ain dear
        Annie.

11. 'What can a woman do, love, I'll do for ye:'
    'Muckle can a woman do, ye canna do for me.'

12. 'Lay about, steer about, lay our ship cannie,
    Do all ye can to save my dear Annie.'

13. 'I've laid about, steer'd about, laid about cannie,
    Our ship's on a sand-bank, she winna sail ony.—

14. 'Ye'll take her in your arms twa, lo, lift her
        cannie,
    And throw her out owre-board, your ain dear
        Annie.'

15. He has ta'en her in his arms twa, lo, lifted her
        cannie,
    He has thrown her out owre-board, his ain dear
        Annie.

16. The corse it did float, the ship it did follow
    Until that they came to the high banks o'
        Yarrow.

17. 'O I'd bury my love on the high banks o'
        Yarrow,
    But the wood it is dear, and the planks they are
        narrow.'

18. He made his love a coffin o' the gowd sae yellow,
    And buried his bonnie love doun in a sea valley.

BROWN ROBYN'S CONFESSION

1. It fell upon a Wadensday
        Brown Robyn's men went to sea;
    But they saw neither moon nor sun
        Nor starlight wi' their e'e.

2. 'We'll cast kevels us amang;
    See wha the man may be.'—
The kevel fell on Brown Robyn,
    The master-man was he.

3. 'It is nae wonder,' said Brown Robyn,
    'Altho' I dinna thrive;
For at home I murder'd my ain father —
    I would he were on live.

4. 'But tie me to a plank o' wude,
    And throw me in the sea;
And if I sink, ye may bid me sink,
    But if I swim, let be.'

5. They've tied him to a plank o' wude
    And thrown him in the sea;
He didna sink, tho' they bade him sink,
    He swim'd, and they bade let be.

6. He hadna been into the sea
    An hour but barely three,
Till by it came Our Blessed Ladie
    Her dear young son her wi'.

7. 'Will ye gang to your men again,
    ·Or will ye gang wi' me?
Will ye gang to the high heavens
    Wi' my dear son and me?'—-

8. 'I winna gang to my men again,
　　For they would be fear'd at me;
　　But I would gang to the high heavens,
　　Wi' thy dear son and thee.'

9. 'It's for nae honour ye did, Brown Robyn,
　　It's for nae gude ye did to me;
　　But a' is for your fair confession
　　You've made upon the sea.'

THE CRUEL MOTHER

1. SHE lean'd her back unto a thorn;
　　Fine flowers in the valley
　And there she has her two babes born,
　　And the green leaves they grow rarely.

2. She's ta'en the ribbon frae her hair,
　And bound their bodies fast and sair.

3. 'Smile na sae sweet, my bonny babes,
　An' ye smile sae sweet, ye'll smile me dead.

4. 'And, O bonny babes, if ye suck sair,
　Ye'll never suck by my side mair.'

5. She's ta'en out her little penknife
　And twinn'd the sweet babes o' their life.

6. She's howket a grave baith deep and wide,
　And there she's buried them side by side.

7. She's buried them baith beneath the brier,
   And washed her hands wi' mony a tear.

8. 'O ay, my God, as I look to thee,
   My babes be atween my God and me!

9. 'And ay their smiles wad win me in,
   But I am borne down by deadly sin.'

10. She's cover'd them o'er wi' a marble stane,
    Thinking she wad gang maiden hame.

11. She lookit out owre her castle wa'
    And saw two naked boys play at the ba'.

12. 'O bonny boys, gin ye were mine
    I wad cleed you in silk and sabelline.

13. 'O I would dress you in the silk,
    And wash you ay in morning milk.'—

14. 'O mother dear, when we were thine,
    You didna prove to us sae kind.

15. 'O cruel mother, we were thine
    And thou made us to wear the twine.

16. 'But now we're in the heavens hie,
    Fine flowers in the valley
    And ye have the pains o' hell to drie'—
    And the green leaves they grow rarely;
    Ten thousand times good night and be wi' thee!

BINNORIE

1. THERE were twa sisters sat in a bour;
   Binnorie, O Binnorie!
   There cam a knight to be their wooer,
   By the bonnie milldams o' Binnorie.

2. He courted the eldest with glove and ring,
   But he lo'ed the youngest abune a' thing.

3. The eldest she was vexèd sair,
   And sair envìed her sister fair.

4. Upon a morning fair and clear,
   She cried upon her sister dear:

5. 'O sister, sister, tak my hand,
   And we'll see our father's ships to land.'

6. She's ta'en her by the lily hand,
   And led her down to the river-strand.

7. The youngest stood upon a stane,
   The eldest cam and push'd her in.

8. 'O sister, sister, reach your hand!
   And ye sall be heir o' half my land:

9. 'O sister, reach me but your glove!
   And sweet William sall be your love.'—

10. 'Foul fa' the hand that I should take;
    It twin'd me o' my warldis make.

11. 'Your cherry cheeks and your yellow hair
    Gar'd me gang maiden evermair.'

12. Sometimes she sank, sometimes she swam,
    Until she cam to the miller's dam.

13. Out then cam the miller's son,
    And saw the fair maid soummin' in.

14. 'O father, father, draw your dam!
    There's either a mermaid or a milk-white
    swan.'

15. The miller hasted and drew his dam,
    And there he found a drown'd womàn.

16. You couldna see her middle sma',
    Her gowden girdle was sae braw.

17. You couldna see her lily feet,
    Her gowden fringes were sae deep.

18. You couldna see her yellow hair
    ·For the strings o' pearls was twisted there.

19. You couldna see her fingers sma',
    Wi' diamond rings they were cover'd a'.

20. And by there cam a harper fine,
    That harpit to the king at dine.

21. And when he look'd that lady on,
    He sigh'd and made a heavy moan.

22. He's made a harp of her breast-bane,
    Whose sound wad melt a heart of stane.

23. He's ta'en three locks o' her yellow hair,
    And wi' them strung his harp sae rare.

24. He went into her father's hall,
    And there was the court assembled all.

25. He laid his harp upon a stane,
    And straight it began to play by lane.

26. 'O yonder sits my father, the King,
    And yonder sits my mother, the Queen;

27. 'And yonder stands my brother Hugh,
    And by him my William, sweet and true.'

28. But the last tune that the harp play'd then —
    Binnorie, O Binnorie!
    Was, 'Woe to my sister, false Helèn!'
    By the bonnie milldams o' Binnorie.

EARL MAR'S DAUGHTER

1. It was intill a pleasant time,
       Upon a simmer's day,
   The noble Earl Mar's daughter
       Went forth to sport and play.

2. And while she play'd and sported
    Below a green aik tree,
  There she saw a sprightly doo
    Set on a tower sae hie.

3. 'O Coo-me-doo, my love sae true,
    If ye'll come doun to me,
  Ye'se hae a cage o' gude red gowd
    Instead o' simple tree.

4. 'I'll put gowd hingers roun' your cage,
    And siller roun' your wa';
  I'll gar ye shine as fair a bird
    As ony o' them a'.'

5. But she had nae these words well spoke,
    Nor yet these words well said,
  Till Coo-me-doo flew frae the tower
    And lichted on her head.

6. Then she has brought this pretty bird
    Hame to her bowers and ha',
  And made him shine as fair a bird
    As ony o' them a'.

7. When day was done, and night was come,
    About the evening-tide,
  This lady spied a gallant youth
    Stand straight up by her side.

8. 'From whence cam' ye, young man?' she
       said;
   'That does surprise me sair;
  My door was bolted right secure,
    What way hae ye come here?'—

9. 'O haud your tongue, ye lady fair,
    Lat a' your folly be;
  Mind ye not o' your turtle-doo
    Ye wiled from aff the tree?'—

10. 'What country come ye frae?' she said,
    'An' what's your pedigree?'—
  'O it was but this verra day
    That I cam' ower the sea.

11. 'My mither lives on foreign isles,
    A queen o' high degree;
  And by her spells I am a doo
    With you to live an' dee.'—

12. 'O Coo-me-doo, my love sae true,
    Nae mair frae me ye'se gae.'—
  That's never my intent, my love;
    As ye said, it shall be sae.'

13. Then he has stay'd in bower wi' her
    For six lang years and ane,
  Till six young sons to him she bare,
    And the seventh she's brought hame.

14. But aye, as ever a child was born,
    He carried them away,
  And brought them to his mither's care
    As fast as he could fly.

15. When he had stay'd in bower wi' her
    For seven lang years an' mair
  There cam' a lord o' high renown
    To court this lady fair.

16. But still his proffer she refused
    And a' his presents too;
  Says, 'I'm content to live alane
    Wi' my bird Coo-me-doo.'

17. Her father swore a michty oath
    Amang the nobles all,
  'The morn, or ere I eat or drink,
    This bird I will gar kill.'

18. The bird was sitting in his cage
    And heard what they did say;
  Says, 'Wae is me, and you forlorn,
    If I do langer stay!'

19. Then Coo-me-doo took flight and flew
    And afar beyond the sea,
  And lichted near his mither's castle
    On a tower o' gowd sae hie.

20. His mither she was walking out
    To see what she could see,
And there she saw her one young son
    Set on the tower sae hie.

21. 'Get dancers here to dance,' she said,
    'And minstrels for to play;
For here's my young son Florentine
    Come hame wi' me to stay.'—

22. 'Get nae dancers to dance, mither,
    Nor minstrels for to play;
For the mither o' my seven sons,
    The morn's her wedding-day.'—

23. 'O tell me, tell me, Florentine,
    Tell me, an' tell me true;
Tell me this day without a flaw
    What I will do for you?'—

24. 'Instead of dancers to dance, mither,
    Or minstrels for to play,
Turn four-and-twenty well-wight men
    Like storks in feathers gray:

25. 'My seven sons in seven swans
    Aboon their heads to flee;
And I mysell a gay goshawk,
    A bird o' high degree.'

26. Then siching said the Queen hersel',
    'That thing's too high for me!'
  But she applied to an auld woman
    Wha had mair skill than she.

27. Instead o' dancers to dance a dance,
    Or minstrels for to play,
  Four-and-twenty well-wight men
    Turn'd birds o' feathers gray.

28. Her seven sons in seven swans,
    Aboon their heads to flee;
  And he himsel' a gay goshawk,
    A bird o' high degree.

29. This flock o' birds took flight and flew
    Beyond the raging sea,
  And landed near the Earl Mar's castle,
    Took shelter in every tree.

30. They were a flock o' pretty birds
    Right comely to be seen;
  The people view'd them wi' surprise
    As they dancèd on the green.

31. These birds flew out frae every tree
    And lichted on the ha',
  And frae the roof with force did flee
    Amang the nobles a'.

32. The storks there seized ilk wedding-guest
    — They could not fight nor flee;
    The swans they bound the bridegroom fast
    Below a green aik tree.

33. They lichted next on the bride-maidens,
    Then on the bride's own head;
    And wi' the twinkling o' an e'e
    The bride an' them were fled.

34. There's ancient men at weddings been
    For sixty years or more,
    But siccan a curious wedding-day
    They never saw before.

35. For naething could the companie do,
    Nor naething could they say;
    But they saw a flock o' pretty birds
    That took their bride away.

PROUD LADY MARGARET

1. FAIR Margret was a proud ladye,
    The King's cousin was she;
    Fair Margret was a rich ladye,
    An' vain as vain cou'd be.

2. Ae night she sat in her stately ha'
    Kaimin' her yellow hair,

When in there cam' a gentle Knight,
   An' a white scarf he did wear.

3. 'O what's your will wi' me, Sir Knight?
   O what's your will wi' me?
You're the likest to my ae brither
   That ever I did see.

4. 'You're the likest to my ae brither
   That ever I hae seen;
But he's buried in Dunfermline kirk
   A month an' mair bygane.'—

5. 'I'm the likest to your ae brither
   That ever ye did see;
But I canna get rest in my grave,
   A' for the pride o' thee.

6. 'Leave pride, Margret, leave pride, Margret,
   Leave pride an' vanity;
Cou'd ye see the sights that I hae seen
   Sair warnèd ye wou'd be.

7. 'For the wee worms are my bedfellows,
   An' cauld clay is my sheets,
An' when the stormy winds do blow
   My body lies and sleeps.

8. 'O ye come in at the kirk-door
   Wi' the red gowd on your crown;

But when you come where I have been,
    You'll wear it laigher down.

9. 'O ye come in at the kirk-door
    Wi' the gowd prins i' your sleeve,
But when you come where I have been
    Ye maun gie them a' their leave.

10. 'Leave pride, Margret, leave pride, Margret,
    Leave pride an' vanity;
Ere ye see the sights that I hae seen,
    Sair alter'd ye maun be.'

11. He got her in her stately ha',
    Kaimin' her yellow hair;
He left her on her sick, sick bed
    Mournin' her sins sae sair.

CLERK SAUNDERS

Part I

1. CLERK SAUNDERS and may Margaret
    Walk'd owre yon garden green;
And deep and heavy was the love
    That fell thir twa between.

2. 'A bed, a bed,' Clerk Saunders said,
    'A bed for you and me!'
'Fye na, fye na,' said may Margaret,
    'Till anes we married be!'—

3. 'Then I'll take the sword frae my scabbard
    And slowly lift the pin;
And you may swear, and save your aith,
    Ye ne'er let Clerk Saunders in.

4. 'Take you a napkin in your hand,
    And tie up baith your bonnie e'en,
And you may swear, and save your aith,
    Ye saw me na since late yestreen.'

5. It was about the midnight hour,
    When they asleep were laid,
When in and came her seven brothers,
    Wi' torches burning red:

6. When in an came her seven brothers,
    Wi' torches burning bright:
They said, 'We hae but one sister,
    And behold her lying with a knight!'

7. Then out and spake the first o' them,
    'I bear the sword shall gar him die.'
And out and spake the second o' them,
    'His father has nae mair but he.'

8. And out and spake the third o' them,
    'I wot that they are lovers dear.'
And out and spake the fourth o' them,
    'They hae been in love this mony a year.'

9. Then out and spake the fifth o' them,
    'It were great sin true love to twain.'
  And out and spake the sixth o' them,
    'It were shame to slay a sleeping man.'

10. Then up and gat the seventh o' them,
    And never a word spake he;
  But he has striped his bright brown brand
    Out through Clerk Saunders' fair bodye.

11. Clerk Saunders he started, and Margaret
    she turn'd
    Into his arms as asleep she lay;
  And sad and silent was the night
    That was atween thir twae.

12. And they lay still and sleepit sound
    Until the day began to daw';
  And kindly she to him did say,
    'It is time, true love, you were awa'.'

13. But he lay still, and sleepit sound,
    Albeit the sun began to sheen;
  She look'd atween her and the wa',
    And dull and drowsie were his e'en.

14. Then in and came her father dear;
    Said, 'Let a' your mourning be;
  I'll carry the dead corse to the clay,
    And I'll come back and comfort thee.'

15. 'Comfort weel your seven sons,
    For comforted I will never be:
  I ween 'twas neither knave nor loon
    Was in the bower last night wi' me.'

PART II

1. The clinking bell gaed through the town,
    To carry the dead corse to the clay;
  And Clerk Saunders stood at may Mar-
        garet's window,
    I wot, an hour before the day.

2. 'Are ye sleeping, Marg'ret?' he says,
    'Or are ye waking presentlie?
  Give me my faith and troth again,
    I wot, true love, I gied to thee.'

3. 'Your faith and troth ye sall never get,
    Nor our true love sall never twin,
  Until ye come within my bower,
    And kiss me cheik and chin.'

4. 'My mouth it is full cold, Marg'ret;
    It has the smell, now, of the ground;
  And if I kiss thy comely mouth,
    Thy days of life will not be lang.

5. 'O cocks are crowing a merry midnight;
    I wot the wild fowls are boding day;

Give me my faith and troth again,
 And let me fare me on my way.'

6. 'Thy faith and troth thou sallna get,
 And our true love sall never twin,
Until ye tell what comes o' women,
 I wot, who die in strong traivelling?'

7. 'Their beds are made in the heavens high,
 Down at the foot of our good Lord's knee,
Weel set about wi' gillyflowers;
 I wot, sweet company for to see.

8. 'O cocks are crowing on merry middle-earth
 I wot the wild fowls are boding day;
'The psalms of heaven will soon be sung,
 And I, ere now, will be miss'd away.'

9. Then she has taken a crystal wand,
 And she has stroken her troth thereon;
She has given it him out at the shot-window
 Wi' mony a sad sigh and heavy groan.

10. 'I thank ye, Marg'ret; I thank ye, Marg'ret;
 And ay I thank ye heartilie;
Gin ever the dead come for the quick,
 Be sure, Marg'ret, I'll come for thee.'

11. It's hosen and shoon, and gown alone,
 She climb'd the wall, and follow'd him,

Until she came to the green forèst,
    And there she lost the sight o' him.

12. 'Is there ony room at your head, Saunders?
    Is there ony room at your feet?
Or ony room at your side, Saunders,
    Where fain, fain, I wad sleep?'

13. 'There's nae room at my head, Marg'ret,
    There's nae room at my feet;
My bed it is fu' lowly now,
    Amang the hungry worms I sleep.

14. 'Cauld mould is my covering now,
    But and my winding-sheet;
The dew it falls nae sooner down
    Than my resting-place is weet.

15. 'But plait a wand o' bonny birk,
    And lay it on my breast;
And shed a tear upon my grave,
    And wish my saul gude rest.'

16. Then up and crew the red, red cock,
    And up and crew the gray:
' 'Tis time, 'tis time, my dear Marg'ret,
    That you were going away.

17. 'And fair Marg'ret, and rare Marg'ret,
    And Marg'ret o' veritie,
Gin e'er ye love another man,
    Ne'er love him as ye did me.'

THE DAEMON LOVER

1. O WHERE hae ye been, my long, long love,
        These seven long years and more?'—
    'O I'm come to seek my former vows,
        That ye promised me before.'—

2. 'Awa' wi' your former vows,' she says,
        'For they will breed but strife;
    Awa' wi' your former vows,' she says,
        'For I am become a wife.

3. 'I am married to a ship-carpenter,
        A ship-carpenter he's bound;
    I wadna he kenn'd my mind this nicht
        For twice five hundred pound.'

4. He turn'd him round and round about,
        And the tear blinded his e'e:
    'I wad never hae trodden on Irish ground
        If it hadna been for thee.

5. 'I might hae had a noble lady,
        Far, far beyond the sea;
    I might hae had a noble lady,
        Were it no for the love o' thee.'—

6. 'If ye might hae had a noble lady,
        Yoursel' ye had to blame;
    Ye might hae taken the noble lady,
        For ye kenn'd that I was nane.'—

7. 'O fause are the vows o' womankind,
    But fair is their fause bodie:
  I wad never hae trodden on Irish ground,
    Were it no for the love o' thee.'—

8. 'If I was to leave my husband dear,
    And my wee young son alsua,
  O what hae ye to tak' me to,
    If with you I should gae?'—

9. 'I hae seven ships upon the sea,
    The eighth brought me to land;
  With mariners and merchandise,
    And music on every hand.

10. 'The ship wherein my love sall sail
    Is glorious to behowd;
  The sails sall be o' the finest silk,
    And the mast o' beaten gowd.'

11. She has taken up her wee young son,
    Kiss'd him baith cheek and chin;
  'O fare ye weel, my wee young son,
    For I'll never see you again!'

12. She has put her foot on gude ship-board,
    And on ship-board she has gane,
  And the veil that hangit ower her face
    Was a' wi' gowd begane.

13. She hadna sail'd a league, a league,
      A league but barely twa,
    Till she minded on her husband she left
      And her wee young son alsua.

14. 'O haud your tongue o' weeping,' he says,
      'Let a' your follies a-bee;
    I'll show where the white lilies grow
      On the banks o' Italie.'

15. She hadna sail'd a league, a league,
      A league but barely three,
    Till grim, grim grew his countenance
      And gurly grew the sea.

16. 'What hills are yon, yon pleasant hills,
      The sun shines sweetly on?'—
    'O yon are the hills o' Heaven,' he said,
      'Where you will never won.'—

17. 'O whaten-a mountain is yon,' she said,
      'Sae dreary wi' frost and snae?'—
    'O yon is the mountain o' Hell,' he said,
      'Where you and I will gae.

18. 'But haud your tongue, my dearest dear,
      Let a' your follies a-bee,
    I'll show where the white lilies grow,
      In the bottom o' the sea.'

19. And aye as she turn'd her round about,
      Aye taller he seem'd to be;
    Until that the tops o' that gallant ship
      Nae taller were than he.

20. He strack the top-mast wi' his hand,
      The fore-mast wi' his knee;
    And he brake that gallant ship in twain,
      And sank her in the sea.

CLERK COLVEN

1. CLERK COLVEN, and his gay ladie,
     As they walk'd in yon garden green,
   The belt about her middle jimp
     It cost Clerk Colven crowns fifteen.

2. 'O hearken weel now, my good lord,
     O hearken weel to what I say;
   When ye gang to the wall o' Stream
     O gang nae near the weel-faur'd may.

3. 'O haud your tongue, my gay ladie,
     Now speak nae mair of that to me;
   For I nae saw a fair woman
     That I cou'd like so well as thee.'

4. He's mounted on his berry-brown steed,
     And merry, merry rade he on,

Till that he came to the wall o' Stream,
And there he saw the mermaiden.

5. 'Ye wash, ye wash, ye bonny may,
   And ay's ye wash your sark o' silk.'—
'It's a' for ye, you gentle knight,
   My skin is whiter than the milk.'

6. He's ta'en her by the milk-white hand,
   He's ta'en her by the sleeve sae green,
And he's forgotten his gay ladie,
   And he's awa' wi' the mermaiden.

7. —'Ohone, alas!' says Clerk Colven,
   'And aye so sair as akes my head!'
And merrily leugh the mermaiden,
   'O 'twill win on till you be dead.

8. 'But out ye tak' your little pen-knife,
   And frae my sark ye shear a gare;
Row that about your lovely head,
   And the pain ye'll never feel nae mair.'

9. Out he has ta'en his little pen-knife,
   And frae her sark he's shorn a gare;
She's ty'd it round his whey-white face,
   But and ay his head it akèd mair.

10. 'Ohone, alas!' says Clerk Colven,
    'O sairer, sairer akes my head!'—

'And sairer, sairer ever will,
  And aye be war' till ye be dead.'

11. Then out he drew his shining blade
      And thought wi' it to be her deid,
    But she's become a fish again,
      And merrily sprang into the fleed.

12. He's mounted on his berry-brown steed,
      And dowie, dowie rade he hame,
    And heavily, heavily lighted down
      When to his ladie's bower he came.

13. 'O mither, mither, mak' my bed,
      And, gentle ladie, lay me down;
    O brither, brither, unbend my bow,
      'Twill never be bent by me again!'

14. His mither she has made his bed,
      His gentle ladie laid him down,
    His brither he has unbent his bow,
      —'Twas never bent by him again.

YOUNG HUNTING

1. 'O LADY, rock never your young son young
      One hour longer for me;
    For I have a sweetheart in Gareloch Wells
      I love thrice better than thee.

2. 'The very sole o' that lady's foot,
    Than thy face is mair white.'—
  'But nevertheless now, Young Hunting,
    Ye'll bide in my bower this night?'

3. She has birl'd in him Young Hunting
    The good ale and the wine,
  Till he was as fou drunken
    As any wild-wood swine.

4. She has kiss'd him by the candle-light
    And the charcoal burning red,
  And up she has ta'en Young Hunting,
    And she's had him to her bed.

5. And she's minded her on a little pen-knife
    That hang'd below her gare,
  And she has gi'en Young Hunting
    A deep wound and a sair.

6. Then up and spake the popinjay
    That flew abune her head:
  'Lady, keep well your green cleiding
    Frae good Young Hunting's bleid!'—

7. 'O better I'll keep my green cleiding
    Frae good Young Hunting's bleid
  Than thou canst keep thy clattering tongue
    That trattles in thy head.'

8. 'O lang, lang is the winter's night,
   And·slowly daws the day!
   There lies a dead man in my bower,
   And I wish he were away.'

9. She has call'd upon her bower-maidens,
   She has call'd them ane by ane:
   'There lies a dead man in my bower,
   I wish that he were gane.'

10. They have booted and spurr'd Young Hunt-
   ing
   As he was wont to ride —
   A hunting-horn about his neck,
   And a sharp sword by his side;
   And they've had him to the wan water,
   Where a' men ca's it Clyde.

11. In the deepest pot of Clyde-water
   It's there they flang him in,
   And put a turf on his breast-bane
   To hold Young Hunting down.

12. Then up and spake the popinjay
   That sat upon the tree;
   'Gae hame, gae hame, ye fause lady,
   And pay your maids their fee.'—

13. 'Come down, come down, my pretty bird,
   That sits upon the tree;

I have a cage o' beaten gold,
    I'll gie it unto thee.'— ·

14. 'How shall I come down, how can I come
        down,
    How shall I come down to thee?
The things ye said to Young Hunting,
    The same ye're saying to me.'

15. She hadna cross'd a rigg o' land,
    A rigg but barely ane,
When she met wi' his auld father,
    Came riding all alane.

16. 'Where has ye been, now, lady fair,
    Where has ye been sae late?
We hae been seeking Young Hunting,
    But him we canna get.'—

17. 'Young Hunting kens a' the fords o' Clyde,
    He'll ride them ane by ane;
And though the night was ne'er so mirk,
    Young Hunting will be hame.'

18. O there came seeking Young Hunting
    Mony a lord and knight,
And there came seeking Young Hunting
    Mony a lady bright.

19. And it fell ance upon a day
    The King was bound to ride,

And he has miss'd Young Hunting,
  Should hae ridden on his right side.

20. And they have to his true love gane;
    But she sware by the thorn,
  'O I have not seen Young Hunting
    Since yesterday at morn.

21. 'It fears me sair in Clyde Water
    That he is drown'd therein!'
  O they have sent for the King's divers,
    To dive for Young Hunting.

22. 'Gar dive, gar dive!' the King he cried,
    'Gar dive for gold and fee!
  O wha will dive for Young Hunting's sake,
    Or wha will dive for me?'

23. They dived in at the tae water-bank,
    They dived in at the tither:
  'We can dive no more for Young Hunting,
    Altho' he were our brither.'

24. It fell that in that lady's castle
    The King was boun to bed,
  And out it spake the popinjay
    That flew abune his head:

25. 'Leave off, leave off, your day diving,
    And dive upon the night;

And where that sackless Knight lies slain
  The candles will burn bright.'

26. They left their diving on the day,
     And dived upon the night;
   And over the place Young Hunting lay
     The candles shone fu' bright.

27. The deepest pot in Clyde Water
     They got Young Hunting in,
   With 'a green turf tied across his breast
     To keep that good lord down.

28. Then up and spake the King himsel',
     When he saw the deadly wound:
   'O wha has slain my right-hand man,
     That held my hawk and hound?'

29. Then up and spake the popinjay,
     Says, 'What needs a' this din?
   It was his light leman took his life,
     And hided him in the linn.'

30. She sware her by the grass sae green,
     So did she by the corn,
   She hadna seen Young Hunting
     Since Monanday at morn.

31. 'Put not the wyte on me,' she says,
     'It was my May Catheren.'

Then they have cut baith thorn and fern, .
   To burn that maiden in.

32. When they had ta'en her May Catheren,
   In the bonfire set her in;
It wouldna take upon her cheeks,
   Nor yet upon her chin,
Nor yet upon her yellow hair,
   To heal the deadly sin.

33. Out they have ta'en her May Catheren,
   And put the lady in:
O it took upon her cheek, her cheek,
   Took fast upon her chin,
Took fast upon her fair body —
   She burnt like hollins green.

THE WIFE OF USHER'S WELL

1. THERE lived a wife at Usher's well,
   And a wealthy wife was she;
She had three stout and stalwart sons,
   And sent them o'er he sea.

2. They hadna been a week from her,
   A week but barely ane,
When word came to the carline wife
   That her three sons were gane.

3. They hadna been a week from her,
   A week but barely three,
   When word came to the carline wife
   That her sons she'd never see.

4. 'I wish the wind may never cease,
   Nor fashes in the flood,
   Till my three sons come hame to me
   In earthly flesh and blood!'

5. It fell about the Martinmas,
   When nights are lang and mirk,
   The carline wife's three sons came hame,
   And their hats were o' the birk.

6. It neither grew in syke nor ditch,
   Nor yet in ony sheugh;
   But at the gates o' Paradise
   That birk grew fair eneugh.

7. 'Blow up the fire, my maidens!
   Bring water from the well!
   For a' my house shall feast this night,
   Since my three sons are well.'

8. And she has made to them a bed,
   She's made it large and wide;
   And she's ta'en her mantle her about,
   Sat down at the bedside.

9. Up then crew the red, red cock,
    And up and crew the gray;
   The eldest to the youngest said,
    ''Tis time we were away.'

10. The cock he hadna craw'd but once,
     And clapp'd his wings at a',
    When the youngest to the eldest said,
     'Brother, we must awa'.

11. 'The cock doth craw, the day doth daw,
     The channerin' worm doth chide;
    Gin we be miss'd out o' our place,
     A sair pain we maun bide.'—

12. 'Lie still, lie still but a little wee while,
     Lie still but if we may;
    Gin my mother should miss us when she
       wakes,
     She'll go mad ere it be day.'—

13. 'Fare ye weel, my mother dear!
     Fareweel to barn and byre!
    And fare ye weel, the bonny lass
     That kindles my mother's fire!'

A LYKE-WAKE DIRGE

1. This ae nighte, this ae nighte,
    — Every nighte and alle,
  Fire and fleet and candle-lighte,
    And Christe receive thy saule.

2. When thou from hence away art past,
    — Every nighte and alle,
  To Whinny-muir thou com'st at last:
    And Christe receive thy saule.

3. If ever thou gavest hosen and shoon,
    — Every nighte and alle,
  Sit thee down and put them on:
    And Christe receive thy saule.

4. If hosen and shoon thou ne'er gav'st nane
    — Every nighte and alle,
  The whinnes sall prick thee to the bare bane;
    And Christe receive thy saule.

5. From whinny-muir when thou may'st pass.
    — Every nighte and alle,
  To Brig o' Dread thou com'st at last;
    And Christe receive thy saule.

6. From Brig o' Dread when thou may'st pass,
    — Every nighte and alle,
  To Purgatory fire thou com'st at last;
    And Christe receive thy saule.

7. If ever thou gavest meat or drink,
     — *Every nighte and alle,*
   The fire sall never make thee shrink;
     And Christe receive thy saule.

8. If meat or drink thou ne'er gav'st nane,
     — *Every nighte and alle,*
   The fire will burn thee to the bare bane;
     And Christe receive thy saule.

9. This ae nighte, this ae nighte,
     — *Every nighte and alle,*
   Fire and fleet and candle-lighte,
     And Christe receive thy saule.

THE UNQUIET GRAVE

1. 'THE wind doth blow to-day, my love,
     And a few small drops of rain;
   I never had but one true-love;
     In cold grave she was lain.

2. 'I'll do as much for my true-love
     As any young man may;
   I'll sit and mourn all at her grave
     For a twelvemonth and a day.'

3. The twelvemonth and a day being up,
     The dead began to speak:

'Oh who sits weeping on my grave,
      And will not let me sleep?'—

4. ''Tis I, my love, sits on your grave,
      And will not let you sleep;
   For I crave one kiss of your clay-cold lips,
      And that is all I seek.'—

5. 'You crave one kiss of my clay-cold lips;
      But my breath smells earthy strong;
   If you have one kiss of my clay-cold lips,
      Your time will not be long.

6. ''Tis down in yonder garden green,
      Love, where we used to walk,
   The finest flower that ere was seen
      Is wither'd to a stalk.

7. 'The stalk is wither'd dry, my love,
      So will our hearts decay;
   So make yourself content, my love,
      Till God calls you away.'

BOOK II

HYND HORN

1. Hynd Horn's bound, love, and Hynd Horn's free,
   With a hey lillelu and a how lo lan;
   Where was ye born, or in what countrie?
   And the birk and the broom blows bonnie.

2. 'In good greenwood, there I was born,
   And all my forbears me beforn.

3. 'O seven long years I served the King,
   And as for wages I never gat nane;

4. 'But ae sight o' his ae daughter.
   And that was thro' an auger-bore.'

5. Seven long years he served the King,
   And it's a' for the sake of his daughter Jean.

6. The King an angry man was he;
   He sent young Hynd Horn to the sea.

7. He's gi'en his luve a silver wand
   Wi' seven silver laverocks sittin' thereon.

8. She's gi'en to him a gay gold ring
   Wi' seven bright diamonds set therein.

69

9. 'As lang's these diamonds keep their hue,
　　Ye'll know I am a lover true:

10. 'But when the ring turns pale and wan,
　　Ye may ken that I love anither man.'

11. He hoist up sails and awa' sail'd he
　　Till that he came to a foreign countrie.

12. One day as he look'd his ring upon,
　　He saw the diamonds pale and wan.

13. He's left the seas and he's come to the land,
　　And the first that he met was an auld beggar man.

14. 'What news, what news? thou auld beggar man,
　　For it's seven years sin I've seen land.'

15. 'No news,' said the beggar, 'no news at a',
　　But there is a wedding in the King's ha'.

16. 'But there is a wedding in the King's ha'
　　That has halden these forty days and twa.'

17. 'Cast off, cast off thy auld beggar weed,
　　And I'll gi'e thee my gude grey steed:

18. 'And lend to me your wig o' hair
　　To cover mine, because it is fair.'—

19. 'My begging weed is na for thee,
　　Your riding steed is na for me.'

20. But part by right and part by wrang
    Hynd Horn has changed wi' the beggar man.

21. The auld beggar man was bound for to ride,
    But young Hynd Horn was bound for the bride.

22. When he came to the King's gate,
    He sought a drink for Hynd Horn's sake.

23. The bride came trippin' down the stair,
    Wi' the scales o' red gowd in her hair;

24. Wi' a cup o' the red wine in her hand,
    And that she gae to the auld beggar man.

25. Out o' the cup he drank the wine,
    And into the cup he dropt the ring.

26. 'O got ye this by sea or land?
    Or got ye it of a dead man's hand?'—

27. 'I got it na by sea nor land,
    But I got it, madam, of your own hand.'

28. 'O, I'll cast off my gowns o' brown,
    And beg with you frae town to town.

29. 'O, I'll cast off my gowns o' red,
    And I'll beg wi' you to win my bread.

30. 'O, I'll take the scales o' gowd frae my hair,
    And I'll follow you for evermair.'

31. She has cast awa' the brown and the red,
    And she's follow'd him to beg her bread.

32. She has ta'en the scales o' gowd frae her hair
    And she's follow'd him for evermair.

33. But atween the kitchen and the ha'
    He has let his cloutie cloak down fa'.

34. And the red gowd shinèd over him a',
    With a hey lillelu, and a how lo lan;
    And the bride frae the bridegroom was stown
        awa',
    And the birk and the broom blows bonnie.

HYND ETIN

1. MAY Margaret sits in her bower door
   Sewing her silken seam;
   She heard a note in Elmond's wood,
   And wish'd she there had been.

2. She loot the seam fa' frae her side,
   The needle to her tae,
   And she is on to Elmond's wood
   As fast as she could gae.

3. She hadna pu'd a nut, a nut,
      Nor broken a branch but ane,
    Till by there came the Hynd Etin,
      Says, 'Lady, lat alane.

4. 'O why pu' ye the nut, the nut,
      Or why break ye the tree?
    For I am forester o' this wood:
      Ye should spier leave at me.'—

5. 'I'll ask leave at nae living man,
      Nor yet will I at thee;
    My father is king o'er a' this realm,
      This wood belongs to me.'

6. The highest tree in Elmond's wood,
      He's pu'd it by the reet,
    And he has built for her a bower
      Near by a hallow seat.

7. He's kept her there in Elmond's wood
      For six lang years and ane,
    Till six pretty sons to him she bare,
      And the seventh she's brought hame.

8. It fell out ance upon a day
      He's to the hunting gane,
    And a' to carry his game for him
      He's tane his eldest son.

9. 'A question I will ask, father,
    Gin ye wadna angry be.'—
  'Say on, say on, my bonny boy,
    Ye'se nae be quarrell'd by me.'

10. 'I see my mither's cheeks aye weet,
    I never can see them dry;
  And I wonder what aileth my mither
    To mourn sae constantly.'—

11. 'Your mither was a king's daughtèr,
    Sprung frae a high degree;
  She might hae wed some worthy prince
    Had she na been stown by me.

12. 'Your mither was a king's daughtèr
    Of noble birth and fame,
  But now she's wife o' Hynd Etin,
    Wha ne'er gat christendame.

13. 'But we'll shoot the buntin' o' the bush,
    The linnet o' the tree,
  And ye'se tak' them hame to your dear
      mither,
    See if she'll merrier be.'

14. It fell upon anither day,
    He's to the hunting gane
  And left his seven young children
    To stay wi' their mither at hame.

15. 'O I will tell to you, mither,
  Gin ye wadna angry be.'—
  'Speak on, speak on, my little wee boy,
   Ye'se nae be quarrell'd by me.'—

16. 'As we came frae the hind-hunting,
  We heard fine music ring.'—
  'My blessings on you, my bonny boy,
   I wish I'd been there my lane.'

17. They wistna weel where they were gaen,
  Wi' the stratlins o' their feet;
  They wistna weel where they were gaen,
   Till at her father's yate.

18. 'I hae nae money in my pocket,
  But royal rings hae three;
  I'll gi'e them you, my little young son,
   And ye'll walk there for me.

19. 'Ye'll gi'e the first to the proud portèr
  And he will let you in;
  Ye'll gi'e the next to the butler-boy
   And he will show you ben;

20. 'Ye'll gi'e the third to the minstrel
  That plays before the King;
  He'll play success to the bonny boy
   Came thro' the wood him lane.'

21. He ga'e the first tc the proud portèr
     And he open'd and let him in;
     He ga'e the next to the butler-boy,
     And he has shown him ben.

22. He ga'e the third to the minstrel
     That play'd before the King,
     And he play'd success to the bonny boy
     Came thro' the wood him lane.

23. Now when he came before the King,
     Fell low upon his knee;
     The King he turn'd him round about,
     And the saut tear blint his e'e.

24. 'Win up, win up, my bonny boy,
     Gang frae my companie;
     Ye look sae like my dear daughtèr,
     My heart will burst in three.'—

25. 'If I look like your dear daughtèr,
     A wonder it is none;
     If I look like your dear daughtèr,
     I am her eldest son.'—

26. 'Will ye tell me, ye little wee boy,
     Where may my Margaret be?'—
     'She's just now standing at your yates,
     And my six brithers her wi'.'—

27. 'O where are a' my porter-boys
        That I pay meat and fee,
    To open my yates baith wide and braid,
        Let her come in to me?'

28. When she cam' in before the King,
        Fell low down on her knee:
    'Win up, win up, my daughter dear,
        This day ye'se dine wi' me.'—

29. 'Ae bit I canna eat, father,
        Nor ae drop can I drink,
    Until I see my mither dear,
        For lang for her I think.'

30. When she cam' in before the queen,
        Fell low down on her knee;
    'Win up, win up, my daughter dear,
        This day ye'se din? wi' me.'—

31. 'Ae bit I canna eat, mither,
        Nor ae drop can I drink,
    Until I see my sister dear,
        For lang for her I think.'

32. When that these twa sisters met,
        She hail'd her courteouslie;
    'Come ben, come ben, my sister dear,
        This day ye'se dine wi' me.'—

33. 'Ae bit I canna eat, sister,
    Nor ae drop can I drink,
Until I see my dear husband,
    So lang for him I think.'—

34. 'O where are a' my rangers bold
    That I pay meat and fee,
To search the forest far an' wide,
    And bring Etin back to me?'

35. Out it speaks the little wee boy:
    'Na, na, this mauna be;
Without ye grant a free pardon,
    I hope ye'll nae him see.'—

36. 'O here I grant a free pardon,
    Well seal'd by my own han';
Ye may mak' search for Young Etin
    As soon as ever ye can.'

37. They search'd the country wide and braid,
    The forest far and near,
And they found him into Elmond's wood,
    Tearing his yellow hair.

38. 'Win up, win up now, Hynd Etin,
    Win up an' boun wi' me;
We're messengers come frae the court;
    The King wants you to see.'—

39. 'O lat them tak' frae me my head,
      Or hang me on a tree;
    For since I've lost my dear lady,
      Life's no pleasure to me.'—

40. 'Your head will na be touch'd, Etin,
      Nor you hang'd on a tree;
    Your lady's in her father's court
      And a' he wants is thee.'

41. When he cam' in before the King,
      Fell low down on his knee;
    'Win up, win up now, Young Etin,
      This day ye'se dine wi' me.'

42. But as they were at dinner set
      The wee boy ask'd a boon:
    'I wish we were in a good kirk
      For to get christendoun.

43. 'For we hae lived in gude green wood
      This seven years and ane;
    But a' this time since e'er I mind
      Was never a kirk within.'—

44. 'Your asking's na sae great, my boy,
      But granted it sall be;
    This day to gude kirk ye sall gang
      And your mither sall gang you wi'.'

45. When unto the gude kirk she came,
     She at the door did stan';
   She was sae sair sunk down wi' shame,
     She couldna come farther ben.

46. Then out and spak' the parish priest,
     And a sweet smile ga'e he:
   'Come ben, come ben, my lily-flower,
     Present your babes to me.'

47. Charles, Vincent, Sam and Dick,
     And likewise John and James;
   They call'd the eldest Young Etin,
     Which was his father's name.

ERLINTON

1. ERLINTON had a fair daughter;
     I wat he wear'd her in a great sin·
   For he has built a bigly bower,
     And a' to put that lady in.

2. An' he has warn'd her sisters six,
     An' sae has he her brethren se'en,
   Outher to watch her a' the night,
     Or else to seek her morn an' e'en.

3. She hadna been i' that bigly bower,
     Na not a night but barely ane,
   Till there was Willie, her ain true love
     Chapp'd at the door, cryin' 'Peace within!'

4. 'O whae is this at my bower door,
    That chaps sae late, nor kens the gin?'—
    'O it is Willie, your ain true love,
    I pray you rise an' let me in.'—

5. 'For a' sae weel as I like ye, Willie,
    For a' sae weel as I ken the gin,
    I wadna for ten thousand pounds, love,
    Na, no this night wad I let ye in.

6. 'But in the green-wood is a wake,
    And at the wake there is a wane,
    An' there I'll come as sune the morn, love,
    Na no a mile but barely ane.

7. 'On my right hand I'll have a glo', love,
    And on my left hand I'll have nane;
    I'll have wi' me my sisters six, love,
    And we will wauk the wood our lane.'

8. Then she's gane to her bed again,
    She has layen till the cock crew thrice,
    An' then she said to her sisters a',
    'Maidens, 'tis time for us to rise.

9. She pat on her back her silken gown,
    An' on her breast a siller pin,
    An' she's ta'en her sisters by the hand,
    An' to the green-wood she is gane.

10. They hadna wauk'd in the bonny green-wood,
    Na no an hour but barely ane,
 Till up start Willie, her ain true love,
    Wha frae her sisters has her ta'en.

11. An' he has kiss'd her sisters six,
    An' he has sent them hame again,
But he has keepit his ain true love,
    Sayin' 'We'll wauk the woods our lane.'

12. They hadna wauk'd in the bonnie green-wood
    Na no an hour but barely ane,
Till up start fifteen o' the bravest outlaws
    That ever bare either blood or bane.

13. Then up bespake the foremost knight,—
    An' O but he spake angrilỳ:
Says, 'Yield to me thy ladye bright,
    This night shall wauk the woods wi' me.'—

14. 'I like her weel, my ladye bright,
    And O my life but it lies me near!
But before I lose my ladye bright
    I'll rather lose my life sae dear.'

15. But up an' spake the second knight —
    I wat he spake right boustruslie —
Says, 'Baith your life an' your ladye bright
    This night shall wauk the woods wi' me.'—

16. 'My ladye is my warldis meed:
    My life I winna yield to nane;
    But if ye be men of your manheid,
      Ye'll only fight me ane by ane.—

17. 'O sit ye down, my dearest dear,
    Sit down an' hold my milk-white steed,
    An' see that ye dinna change your cheer
      Until ye see my body bleed.'

18. He set his back unto an aik,
    He set his feet against a stane,
    He's feightin' a' these fifteen outlaws,
      An' kill'd them a' but barely ane.

19. An' he has gane to his ladye dear,
    I wat he kiss'd her cheek an' chin —
    'Thou art mine ain, I have bought thee dear,
      An' now we will wauk the woods our lane.'

THE DOUGLAS TRAGEDY

1. 'RISE up, rise up now, Lord Douglas,' she says,
    'And put on your armour so bright;
    Let it never be said that a daughter of thine
      Was married to a lord under night.

2. 'Rise up, rise up, my seven bold sons,
    And put on your armour so bright,

And take better care of your youngest sister,
    For your eldest's awa the last night.'

3. He's mounted her on a milk-white steed,
    And himself on a dapple grey,
With a bugelet horn hung down his side;
    And lightly they rode away.

4. Lord William look'd o'er his left shoulder,
    To see what he could see,
And there he spy'd her seven brethren bold
    Come riding over the lea.

5. 'Light down, light down, Lady Margret,' he said,
    'And hold my steed in your hand,
Until that against your seven brethren bold,
    And your father, I mak' a stand.'

6. O, there she stood, and bitter she stood,
    And never did shed one tear,
Until that she saw her seven brethren fa',
    And her father, who lov'd her so dear.

7. 'O hold your hand, Lord William!' she said,
    'For your strokes they are wondrous sair;
True lovers I can get many an ane,
    But a father I can never get mair.'

8. O she's ta'en out her handkerchief,
    It was o' the holland sae fine,

And aye she dighted her father's wounds,
    That were redder than the wine.

9. 'O chuse, O chuse, Lady Margret,' he said,
    'O whether will ye gang or bide?'
  'I'll gang, I'll gang, Lord William,' she said,
    'For ye've left me no other guide.'

10. He's lifted her on a milk-white steed,
    And himself on a dapple grey,
  With a bugelet horn hung down by his side;
    And slowly they baith rade away.

11. O they rade on, and on they rade,
    And a' by the light of the moon,
  Until they came to yon wan water,
    And there they lighted doun.

12. They lighted doun to tak' a drink
    Of the spring that ran sae clear,
  And doun the stream ran his gude heart's
      blood,
    And sair she gan to fear.

13. 'Hold up, hold up, Lord William,' she says,
    'For I fear that you are slain.'—
  ''Tis naething but the shadow of my scarlet
      cloak,
    That shines in the water sae plain.'

14. O they rade on, and on they rade,
  And a' by the light of the moon,
 Until they cam' to his mother's ha' door,
  And there they lighted doun.

15. Get up, get up, lady mother,' he says,
  'Get up, and let me in!
 'Get up, get up, lady mother,' he says,
  'For this night my fair lady I've win.

16. 'O mak my bed, lady mother,' he says,
  'O mak it braid and deep,
 And lay Lady Margret close at my back,
  And the sounder I will sleep.'

17. Lord William was dead lang ere midnight,
  Lady Margret lang ere day,
 And all true lovers that go thegither,
  May they have mair luck than they!

18. Lord William was buried in St. Mary's kirk,
  Lady Margret in Mary's quire;
 Out o' the lady's grave grew a bonny red rose,
  And out o' the knight's a brier.

19. And they twa met, and they twa plat,
  And fain they wad be near;
 And a' the warld might ken right weel
  They were twa lovers dear.

20. But bye and rade the Black Douglas,
 And wow but he was rough!
For he pull'd up the bonny brier,
 And flang 't in St. Mary's Lough.

GLASGERION

1. GLASGERION was a King's own son,
 And a harper he was good;
He harpèd in the King's chamber
 Where cup and candle stood,
And so did he in the Queen's chamber,
 Till ladies waxèd wood.

2. And then bespake the King's daughter
 And these words thus said she:
'There's never a stroke comes over this harp,
 But it glads the heart of me.'

3. Said, 'Strike on, strike on, Glasgerion,
 Of thy striking do not blin;
There's never a stroke comes over thine harp
 But it glads my heart within.'

4. 'Fair might you fall, lady,' quoth he;
 'Who taught you now to speak?
I have loved you, lady, seven year;
 My. heart I durst ne'er break.'—

5. 'But come to my bower, my Glasgerion,
    When all men are at rest;
  As I am a lady true of my promise,
    Thou shalt be a welcome guest.'

6. But home then came Glasgerion,
    A glad man, Lord, was he!
  'And come thou hither, Jack, my boy,
    Come hither unto me.

7. 'For the King's daughter of Normandye
    Her love is granted me;
  And before the cock have crowen
    At her chamber must I be.'

8. 'But come you hither, master,' quoth he,
    'Lay your head down on this stone;
  For I will waken you, master dear,
    Afore it be time to gone.'

9. But up then rose that lither lad,
    And did on hose and shoon;
  A collar he cast upon his neck,
    He seemèd a gentleman.

10. And when he came to that lady's chamber
    He tirl'd upon a pin;
  The lady was true of her promise,
    Rose up and let him in.

11. He did not kiss that lady gay
    When he came nor when he yode;
    And sore mistrusted that lady gay
    He was of some churle's blood.

12. But home then came that lither lad,
    And did off his hose and shoon,
    And cast that collar from 'bout his neck;
    He was but a churlè's son:
    'Awaken,' quoth he, 'my master dear,
    I hold it time to be gone.

13. 'For I have saddled your horse, master,
    Well bridled I have your steed;
    Have not I served a good breakfast
    When time comes I have need?'

14. But up then rose good Glasgerion,
    And did on both hose and shoon,
    And cast a collar about his neck;
    He was a Kingé's son.

15. And when he came to that lady's chamber,
    He tirl'd upon a pin;
    The lady was more than true of her promise,
    Rose up, and let him in.

16. Says, 'Whether have you left with me
    Your bracelet or your glove?
    Or are you back return'd again
    To know more of my love?'

17. Glasgerion swore a full great oath
    By oak and ash and thorn,
 'Lady, I was never in your chamber
    Sith the time that I was born.'—

18. 'O then it was your little foot-page
    Falsely hath beguiled me:'
 And then she pull'd forth a little pen-knife
    That hangèd by her knee,
 Says, 'There shall never no churlè's blood
    Spring within my bodye.'

19. But home then went Glasgerion,
    A woe man, Lord, was he;
 Sayes, 'Come hither, thou Jack, my boy,
    Come thou hither to me.

20. 'For if I had kill'd a man to-night,
    Jack, I would tell it thee,
 But if I have not kill'd a man to-night,
    Jack, thou hast killéd three!'

21. And he pull'd out his bright brown sword,
    And dried it on his sleeve,
 And he smote off that lither lad's head
    And ask'd no man no leave.

22. He set the sword's point till his breast,
    The pommel till a stone;
 Through the falseness of that lither lad
    These three lives wern all gone.

FAIR ANNIE

1. 'It's narrow, narrow, mak your bed,
     And learn to lie your lane;
   For I'm gaun owre the sea, Fair Annie,
     A braw Bride to bring hame.
   Wi' her I will get gowd and gear,
     Wi' you I ne'er gat nane.

2. 'But wha will bake my bridal bread,
     Or brew my bridal ale?
   And wha will become my bright Bride,
     That I bring owre the dale?'—

3. 'It's I will bake your bridal bread,
     And brew your bridal ale;
   And I will welcome your bright Bride,
     That you bring owre the dale.'—

4. 'But she that welcomes my bright Bride
     Maun gang like maiden fair;
   She maun lace on her robe sae jimp,
     And comely braid her hair.

5. 'Bind up, bind up your yellow hair,
     And tie it on your neck;
   And see you look as maiden-like
     As the day that first we met.'—

6. 'O how can I gang maiden-like,
     When maiden I am nane?

Have I not borne six sons to thee,
    And am wi' child again?'—

7. 'I'll put cooks into my kitchen,
    And stewards in my hall,
And I'll have bakers for my bread,
    And brewers for my ale;
But you're to welcome my bright Bride,
    That I bring owre the dale.'

8. Three months and a day were gane and past
    Fair Annie she gat word
That her love's ship was come at last,
    Wi' his bright young Bride aboard.

9. She's ta'en her young son in her arms,
    Anither in her hand;
And she's gane up to the highest tower,
    Looks over sea and land.

10. 'Come doun, come doun, my mother dear,
    Come aff the castle wa'!
I fear if langer ye stand there,
    Ye'll let yoursell doun fa'.'

11. She's ta'en a cake o' the best bread,
    A stoup o' the best wine,
And a' the keys upon her arm,
    And to the yett is gane.

12. 'O ye're welcome hame, my ain gude lord,
    To your castles and your towers;
  Ye're welcome hame, my ain gude lord,
    To your ha's, but and your bowers.
  And welcome to your hame, fair lady!
    For a' that's here is yours.'

13. 'O whatna lady's that, my lord,
    That welcomes you and me?
  Gin I be lang about this place,
    Her friend I mean to be.'

14. Fair Annie served the lang tables
    Wi' the white bread and the wine;
  But ay she drank the wan water
    To keep her colour fine.

15. And aye she served the lang tables
    Wi' the white bread and the brown,
  And aye she turn'd her round about,
    Sae fast the tears fell doun.

16. She took a napkin lang and white,
    And hung it on a pin;
  It was to wipe away the tears,
    As she gaed out and in.

17. When bells were rung and mass was sung,
    And a' men bound for bed,
  The bridegroom and the bonny Bride
    In ae chamber were laid.

18. Fair Annie's ta'en a harp in her hand,
    To harp thir twa asleep;
    But ay, as she harpit and she sang,
    Fu' sairly did she weep.

19. 'O gin my sons were seven rats,
    Rinnin' on the castle wa',
    And I mysell a great grey cat,
    I soon wad worry them a'!

20. 'O gin my sons were seven hares,
    Rinnin' owre yon lily lea,
    And I mysell a good greyhound,
    Soon worried they a' should be!'

21. Then out and spak the bonny young Bride,
    In bride-bed where she lay:
    'That's like my sister Annie,' she says:
    'Wha is it doth sing and play?

22. 'I'll put on my gown,' said the new-come
    Bride,
    'And my shoes upon my feet;
    I will see wha doth sae sadly sing,
    And what is it gars her greet.

23. 'What ails you, what ails you, my house-
    keeper,
    That ye mak sic a mane?
    Has ony wine-barrel cast its girds,
    Or is a' your white bread gane?'—

24. 'It isna because my wine is spilt,
     Or that my white bread's gane;
     But because I've lost my true love's love,
     And he's wed to anither ane.'—

25. 'Noo tell me wha was your father?' she
          says,
     'Noo tell me wha was your mither?
     And had ye ony sister?' she says,
     'And had ye ever a brither?'—

26. 'The Earl of Wemyss was my father,
     The Countess of Wemyss my mither,
     Young Elinor she was my sister dear,
     And Lord John he was my brither.'—

27. 'If the Earl of Wemyss was your father,
     I wot sae was he mine;
     And it's O my sister Annie!
     Your love ye sallna tyne.

28. 'Tak your husband, my sister dear;
     You ne'er were wrang'd for me,
     Beyond a kiss o' his merry mouth
     As we cam owre the sea.

29. 'Seven ships, loaded weel,
     Cam owre the sea wi' me;
     Ane o' them will tak me hame,
     And six I'll gie to thee.'

THE LASS OF LOCHROYAN

1. 'O WHA will shoe my bonny foot?
     And wha will glove my hand?
   And wha will bind my middle jimp
     Wi' a lang, lang linen band?

2. 'O wha will kame my yellow hair,
     With a haw bayberry kame?
   And wha will be my babe's father
     Till Gregory come hame?'—

3. 'Thy father, he will shoe thy foot,
     Thy brother will glove thy hand,
   Thy mither will bind thy middle jimp
     Wi' a lang, lang linen band.

4. 'Thy sister will kame thy yellow hair,
     Wi' a haw bayberry kame;
   The Almighty will be thy babe's father
     Till Gregory come hame.'—

5. 'And wha will build a bonny ship,
     And set it on the sea?
   For I will go to seek my love,
     My ain love Gregory.'

6. Up then spak her father dear,
     A wafu' man was he;
   'And I will build a bonny ship,
     And set her on the sea.

7. 'And I will build a bonny ship,
      And set her on the sea,
   And ye sal gae and seek your love,
      Your ain love Gregory.'

8. Then he's gart build a bonny ship,
      And set it on the sea,
   Wi' four-and-twenty mariners,
      To bear her company.

9. O he's gart build a bonny ship,
      To sail on the salt sea;
   The mast was o' the beaten gold,
      The sails o' cramoisie.

10. The sides were o' the gude stout aik,
       The deck o' mountain pine,
    The anchor o' the silver shene,
       The ropes o' silken twine.

11. She hadna sail'd but twenty leagues,
       But twenty leagues and three,
    When she met wi' a rank reiver,
       And a' his companie.

12. 'Now are ye Queen of Heaven hie,
       Come to pardon a' our sin?
    Or are ye Mary Magdalane,
       Was born at Bethlehem?'—

13. 'I'm no the Queen of Heaven hie,
      Come to pardon ye your sin,
    Nor am I Mary Magdalane,
      Was born in Bethlehem.

14. 'But I'm the lass of Lochroyan,
      That's sailing on the sea
    To see if I can find my love,
      My ain love Gregory.'—

15. 'O see na ye yon bonny bower?
      It's a' covered owre wi' tin?
    When thou hast sail'd it round about,
      Lord Gregory is within.'

16. And when she saw the stately tower,
      Shining both clear and bright,
    Whilk stood aboon the jawing wave,
      Built on a rock of height,

17. Says, 'Row the boat, my mariners,
      And bring me to the land,
    For yonder I see my love's castle,
      Close by the salt sea strand.'

18. She sail'd it round, and sail'd it round,
      And loud and loud cried she,
    'Now break, now break your fairy charms
      And set my true-love free!'

19. She's ta'en her young son in her arms,
    And to the door she's gane,
  And long she knock'd, and sair she ca'd,
    But answer got she nane.

20. 'O open, open, Gregory!
    O open! if ye be within;
  For here's the lass of Lochroyan,
    Come far fra kith and kin.

21. 'O open the door, Lord Gregory!
    O open and let me in!
  The wind blows loud and cauld, Gregory,
    The rain drops fra my chin.

22. 'The shoe is frozen to my foot,
    The glove unto my hand,
  The wet drops fra my yellow hair,
    Na langer dow I stand.'

23. O up then spak his ill mither,
    — An ill death may she die!
  'Ye're no the lass of Lochroyan,
    She's far out-owre the sea.

24. 'Awa', awa', ye ill woman,
    Ye're no come here for gude;
  Ye're but some witch or wil' warlock,
    Or mermaid o' the flood.'—

25. 'I am neither witch nor wil' warlock,
      Nor mermaid o' the sea,
    But I am Annie of Lochroyan,
      O open the door to me!'—

26. 'Gin ye be Annie of Lochroyan,
      As I trow thou binna she,
    Now tell me of some love-tokens
      That pass'd 'tween thee and me.'

27. 'O dinna ye mind, love Gregory,
      As we sat at the wine,
    We changed the rings frae our fingers?
      And I can shew thee thine.

28. 'O yours was gude, and gude enough,
      But ay the best was mine,
    For yours was o' the gude red gowd,
      But mine o' the diamond fine.

29. 'Yours was o' the gude red gowd,
      Mine o' the diamond fine;
    Mine was o' the purest troth,
      But thine was false within.'—

30. 'If ye be the lass of Lochroyan,
      As I kenna thou be,
    Tell me some mair o' the love-tokens
      Pass'd between thee and me.'—

31. 'And dinna ye mind, love Gregory!
    As we sat on the hill,
Thou twin'd me o' my maidenheid,
    Right sair against my will?

32. 'Now open the door, love Gregory!
    Open the door! I pray;
For thy young son is in my arms,
    And will be dead ere day.'—

33. 'Ye lie, ye lie, ye ill woman,
    So loud I hear ye lie;
For Annie of the Lochroyan
    Is far out-owre the sea.'

34. Fair Annie turn'd her round about:
    'Weel, sine that it be sae,
May ne'er woman that has borne a son
    Hae a heart sae fu' o' wae!

35. 'Tak down, tak down that mast o' gowd,
    Set up a mast of tree;
It disna become a forsaken lady
    To sail sae royallie.'

36. When the cock had crawn, and the day
        did dawn,
    And the sun began to peep,
Up then raise Lord Gregory,
    And sair, sair did he weep.

37. 'O I hae dream'd a dream, mither,
 I wish it may bring good!
 That the bonny lass of Lochroyan
  At my bower window stood.

38. 'O I hae dream'd a dream, mither,
 The thought o't gars me greet!
 That fair Annie of Lochroyan
  Lay dead at my bed-feet.'—

39. 'Gin it be for Annie of Lochroyan
 That ye mak a' this mane,
 She stood last night at your bower-door,
  But I hae sent her hame.'—

40. 'O wae betide ye, ill woman,
 An ill death may ye die!
 That wadna open the door yoursell
  Nor yet wad waken me.'

41. O he's gane down to yon shore-side,
 As fast as he could dree,
 And there he saw fair Annie's bark
  A rowing owre the sea.

42. 'O Annie, Annie,' loud he cried,
 'O Annie, O Annie, bide!'
 But ay the mair he cried 'Annie,'
  The braider grew the tide.

43. 'O Annie, Annie, dear Annie,
      Dear Annie, speak to me!'
    But ay the louder he 'gan call,
      The louder roar'd the sea.

44. The wind blew loud, the waves rose hie
      And dash'd the boat on shore;
    Fair Annie's corpse was in the faem,
      The babe rose never more.

45. Lord Gregory tore his gowden locks
      And made a wafu' moan;
    Fair Annie's corpse lay at his feet,
      His bonny son was gone.

46. O cherry, cherry was her cheek,
      And gowden was her hair,
    And coral, coral was her lips,
      Nane might with her compare!

47. Then first he kiss'd her pale, pale cheek,
      And syne he kiss'd her chin,
    And syne he kiss'd her wane, wane lips,
      There was na breath within.

48. 'O wae betide my ill mither,
      An ill death may she die!
    She turn'd my true-love frae my door,
      Who cam so far to me.

49. 'O wae betide my ill mither,
      An ill death may she die!
    She has no been the deid o' ane,
      But she's been the deid of three.'

50. Then he's ta'en out a little dart,
      Hung low down by his gore,
    He thrust it through and through his heart,
      And words spak never more.

YOUNG BEICHAN

1. In London was Young Beichan born,
     He long'd strange countries for to see;
   But he was ta'en by a savage Moor
     Who handled him right cruellie.

2. For he view'd the fashions of that land,
     Their way of worship viewèd he;
   But to Mahound or Termagant
     Would Beichan never bend a knee.

3. So thro' every shoulder they've bored a bore,
     And thro' every bore they've putten a tree
   And they have made him trail the wine
     And spices on his fair bodie.

4. They've casten him in a dungeon deep,
     Where he could neither hear nor see;
   And fed him on nought but bread and water
     Till he for hunger's like to die.

5. This Moor he had but ae daughter,
    Her name was callèd Susie Pye,
  And every day as she took the air
    She heard Young Beichan sadly crie:

6. 'My hounds they all run masterless,
    My hawks they flie from tree to tree,
  My youngest brother will heir my lands;
    Fair England again I'll never see!

7. 'O were I free as I hae been,
    And my ship swimming once more on sea,
  I'd turn my face to fair England
    And sail no more to a strange countrie!'

8. Young Beichan's song for thinking on
    All night she never closed her e'e;
  She's stown the keys from her father's head
    Wi' mickle gold and white monie.

9. And she has open'd the prison doors:
    I wot she open'd twa or three
  Ere she could come Young Beichan at,
    He was lock'd up so curiouslie.

10. 'O hae ye any lands or rents,
    Or cities in your own countrie,
  Cou'd free you out of prison strong
    And cou'd maintain a lady free?'—

11. 'O London city is my own,
   And other cities twa or three;
   I'll give them all to the lady fair
   That out of prison will set me free.'

12. O she has bribed her father's men
   Wi' mickle gold and white monie,
   She's gotten the keys of the prison strong,
   And she has set Young Beichan free.

13. She's fed him upon the good spice-cake,
   The Spanish wine and the malvoisie;
   She's broken a ring from off her finger
   And to Beichan half of it gave she.

14. 'Go set your foot on good ship-board,
   And haste you back to your own countrie,
   But before that seven years has an end,
   Come back again, love, and marry me.'

15. It was long or seven years had an end
   She long'd full sore her love to see;
   So she's set her foot on good ship-board
   And turn'd her back on her own countrie.

16. She's sailèd east, she's sailèd west,
   She's sailèd all across the sea,
   And when she came to fair England
   The bells were ringing merrilie.

17. 'O whose are a' yon flock o' sheep?
     And whose are a' yon flock o' kye?
     And whose are a' yon pretty castles,
         That I so often do pass by?'

18. 'O they are a' Lord Beichan's sheep,
         And they are a' Lord Beichan's kye,
     And they are a' Lord Beichan's castles
         That you so often do pass by.

19. 'O there's a wedding in yonder ha',
         Has lasted thirty days and three;
     Lord Beichan will not bed wi' his bride
         For love of one that's 'yond the sea.'

20. When she came to Young Beichan's gate
         She tirlèd softly at the pin;
     So ready was the proud portèr
         To open and let this lady in.

21. 'Is this Young Beichan's gates?' she says,
         'Or is that noble lord within?'—
     'He's up the stairs wi' his bonny bride,
         For this is the day o' his weddin'.'—

22. 'O has he taken a bonny bride,
         And has he clean forgotten me?'
     And sighing said that ladye gay,
         'I wish I were in my own countrie!'

23. She's putten her hands in her pockèt
    And gi'en the porter guineas three;
    Says, 'Take ye that, ye proud portèr,
    And bid the bridegroom speak with me.'

24. And she has ta'en her gay gold ring,
    That with her love she brake so free;
    Says, 'Gie him that, ye proud portèr,
    And bid the bridegroom speak with me.'

25. O when the porter came up the stair,
    He's kneelèd low upon his knee:
    'Won up, won up, ye proud portèr,
    And what makes a' this courtesie?'—

26. 'O I've been porter at your gates
    I'm sure this thirty years and three,
    But there is a lady stands thereat
    The fairest I did ever see.'

27. It's out then e thspake bride's mother,
    — Aye, and an angry woman was she —
    'Ye might have excepted our bonny bride,
    And twa or three of our companie.'

28. 'My dame, your daughter's fair enough,
    And aye the fairer mote she be!
    But the fairest time that ever she was,
    She'll no compare wi' this ladye.

29. 'For on every finger she has a ring,
    And on the mid-finger she has three,
    And as mickle gold she has on her brow
        'Would buy an earldome o' land to me.

30. 'And this golden ring that's broken in twa,
    She sends the half o' this golden ring,
    And bids you speak with a lady fair,
    That out o' prison did you bring.'

31. Then up and started Young Beichan
    And sware so loud by Our Ladye,
    'It can be none but Susie Pye,
    That has come over the sea to me!

32. O quickly ran he down the stair,
    Of fifteen steps he made but three;
    He's ta'en his bonny love in his arms
    And kiss'd and kiss'd her tenderlie.

33. 'O have ye ta'en another bride,
    And have ye quite forsaken me?
    And have ye clean forgotten her
    That gave you life and libertie?'

34. She's lookèd over her left shoulder
    To hide the tears stood in her e'e;
    'Now fare-thee-well, Young Beichan,' she
        says,
    'I'll strive to think no more on thee.'

35. 'O never, never, Susie Pye,
  For surely this can never be,
 That ever I shall wed but her
  That's done and dreed so much for me!'

36. Then up bespake the bride's mother —
  She never was heard to speak so free:
 'Ye'll not forsake my only daughter,
  Though Susie Pye has cross'd the sea.'

37. 'Take home, take home your daughter,
   madam,
  She's never a bit the worse for me;
 For saving a kiss of her bonny lips
  Of your daughter's body I am free.'

38. He's ta'en her by the milk-white hand
  And led her to yon fountain-stone;
 He's changed her name from Susie Pye
  And call'd her his bonny love Lady Joan.

CHILDE MAURICE

1. CHILDE MAURICE hunted the Silver Wood,
  He whistled and he sang:
 'I think I see the woman yonder
  That I have lovèd lang.'

2. He callèd to his little man John,
   'You don't see what I see;
For yonder I see the very first woman
   That ever lovèd me.'

3. He says, 'Come hither, my little man John,
   That I pay meat and fee,
For thou shalt go to John Steward's wife
   And greet her well from me;

4. 'And as it falls as many times
   As knots be knit in a kell,
Or merchantmen go to leeve Londòn
   To buy ware or to sell;

5. 'And as it falls as many times
   As any heart can think,
Or school-masters are in any school
   Writing with pen and ink.

6. 'Here is a glove, a glove,' he says,
   'Lined wi' the silver-gris;
Bid her to come to Silver Wood
   To speak with Childe Maurice.

7. 'And here is a ring, a ring,' he says,
   'A ring of the precious stone:
He prays her come to Silver Wood
   And ask the leave of none.'—

8. 'Well do I love your errand, master,
But better I love my life.
Would ye have me go to John Steward's castle,
To tryst away his wife?'—

9. 'Do not I give you meat?' he says,
'Do not I give you fee?
How daur you stop my errand
When that I bid you flee?'

10. This little man John one while he yode,
Another while he ran;
Until he came to John Steward's castle
I wis he never blan.

11. He ask'd no porter's leave, but ran
Up hall and bower free,
And when he came to John Steward's wife,
Says, 'God you save and see!

12. 'I come, I am come from Childe Maurice —
A message unto thee!
And Childe Maurice he greets you well,
And ever so well from me,

13. 'And as it falls as oftentimes
As knots be knit in a kell,
Or merchantmen go to leeve Londòn
To buy ware or to sell;

14. 'And as oftentimes he greets you well
    As any heart can think,
  Or schoolmasters are in any school
    Writing with pen and ink.

15. 'Here is a glove, a glove,' he says,
    'Lined wi' the silver-gris;
  Ye're bidden to come to Silver Wood
    To speak with Childe Maurice.

16. 'And here is a ring, a ring of gold,
    Set wi' the precious stone:
  He prays you to come to Silver Wood
    And ask the leave of none.'—

17. 'Now peace, now peace, thou little man John,
    For Christ's sake I pray thee!
  For gif my lord heard one o' thy words
    Thou must be hangèd hie!'

18. O aye she stampèd with her foot
    And winkèd with her e'e;
  But for all that she could say or do
    Forbidden he would not be.

19. 'It's surely to my bower-woman,
    It cannot be to me!'—
  'Nay, I brought it to John Steward's lady,
    And I trow that thou art she.'

20. Out then spake the wily nurse,
    Wi' the bairn just on her knee:
    'If this be come from Childe Maurice
    It's dear welcome to me.'—

21. 'Thou liest, thou liest, thou wily nurse,
    So loud as I hear thee lie!
    I brought it to John Steward's lady,
    And I trow thou be not she.'

22. Then up and rose him John Steward,
    And an angry man was he:
    'Did I think there was a lord in the world
    My lady loved but me!'

23. He struck the table wi' his foot,
    And kepp'd it with his knee,
    Till silver cup and ezar dish
    In flinders they did flee.

24. He call'd unto his horse-keeper,
    'Make ready you my steed!'
    So did he to his chamberlain,
    'Go fetch my lady's weed!'

25. O he dress'd himself in the holland smock,
    The mantle and the snood,
    And he cast a lease upon his back,
    And he rode to Silver Wood.

26. And when he came to Silver Wood,
        No body saw he there
    But Childe Maurice upon a block
        Combing his yellow hair.

27. Childe Maurice sat in Silver Wood,
        He whistled and he sang:
    'I think I see the woman come
        That I have lovèd lang.'

28. But then stood up him Childe Maurice
        His mother to help from horse:
    'O alas, alas!' says Childe Maurice,
        'My mother was ne'er so gross!'

29. 'No wonder, no wonder,' John Steward he
            said,
        'My lady loved thee well,
    For the fairest part of my body
        Is blacker than thy heel.'

30. John Steward had a little brown sword
        That hung low down by his knee;
    He has cut the head off Childe Maurice
        And the body put on a tree.

31. And he prick'd the head on his sword's point,
        Went singing there beside,
    And he rode till he came to the castle
        Whereas his lady ly'ed.

32. And when he came to his lady —
    Look'd o'er the castle-wall —
    He threw the head into her lap,
    Saying 'Lady, tak' the ball!'

33. Says, 'Dost thou know Childe Maurice' head,
    If that thou dost it see?
    And lap it soft, and kiss it oft,
    For thou loved'st him better than me.'

34. But when she look'd on Childe Maurice' head
    She ne'er spake words but three:
    'I never bare no child but one,
    And you have slain him, trulye.'

35. And she has taken the bloody head
    And kiss'd it, cheek and chin:
    'I was once as full o' Childe Maurice
    As the hip is o' the stane.

36. 'I got him in my mother's bower
    Wi' mickle sin and shame;
    I brought him up in the good greenwood
    Under the shower and rain.'

37. And she has taken her Childe Maurice
    And kiss'd him, mouth and chin:
    'O better I love my Childe Maurice
    Than all my royal kin!'

38. 'Woe be to thee!' John Steward he said,
    And a woe, woe man was he;
    'For if you had told me he was your son,
    He had never been slain by me.'

39. Says, 'Wicked be my merry men all,
    I gave meat, drink and cloth!
    But could they not have holden me
    When I was in all that wrath?'

BROWN ADAM

1. O WHA would wish the wind to blau
   Or the green leaves fa' therewith?
   Or wha would wish a lealer love
   Than Brown Adam the Smith?

2. But they hae banish'd Brown Adam,
   Frae father and frae mither;
   And they hae banish'd Brown Adam,
   Frae sister and frae brither.

3. And they hae banish'd Brown Adam
   Frae the flow'r o' a' his kin;
   And he's biggit a bow'r i' the good green-wood
   Between his ladye and him.

4. O it fell once upon a day
   Brown Adam he thought long,
And he is to the green-wood
   As fast as he could gang.

5. He has ta'en his bow his arm over,
   His sword intill his han',
And he is to the good green-wood
   To hunt some venison.   .

6. O he's shot up, and he's shot down
   The bunting on the breer;
And he's sent it hame to his ladye,
   Bade her be of good cheer.

7. O he's shot up, and he's shot down,
   ·The linnet on the thorn,
And sent it hame to his ladye,
   Said he'd be hame the morn.

8. When he cam' till his lady's bow'r-door
   He stood a little forbye,
And there he heard a fu' fause knight
   Tempting his gay ladye.

9. O he's ta'en out a gay gold ring
   Had cost him mony a poun';
'O grant me love for love, ladye,
   And this sall be your own.'—

10. 'I lo'e Brown Adam well,' she says,
    'I wot sae does he me;
  I wadna gie Brown Adam's love
    For nae fause knight I see.'

11. Out he has ta'en a purse of gold
    Was a' fu' to the string;
  'O grant me love for love, ladye,
    And a' this sall be thine.'—

12. 'I lo'e Brown Adam well,' she says,
    'An' I ken sae does he me;
  An' I wadna be your light leman
    For mair nor ye could gie.'

13. Then out he drew his lang, lang bran',
    And he's flash'd it in her e'en:
  'Now grant me love for love, lady,
    Or thro' you this sall gang.'—

14. 'O,' sighing said this gay ladye,
    'Brown Adam tarries lang!'—
  Then up and starts him Brown Adam,
    Says, 'I'm just to your hand.'

15. He's gar'd him leave his bow, his bow,
    He's gar'd him leave his brand;
  He's gar'd him leave a better pledge —
    Four fingers o' his right hand.

LITTLE MUSGRAVE AND LADY BARNARD

> *O wow for day!*
> *And, dear, gin it were day!*
> *Gin it were day, and I were away —*
> *For I ha' na lang time to stay.*

1. As it fell on one holy-day,
   As many be in the year,
   When young men and maids together did go
   Their matins and mass to hear,

2. Little Musgrave came to the church-door —
   The priest was at private mass —
   But he had more mind of the fair women
   Than he had of Our Lady's grace.

3. The one of them was clad in green,
   Another was clad in pall,
   And then came in my Lord Barnard's wife,
   The fairest amongst them all.

4. She cast an eye on Little Musgrave
   As bright as the summer sun;
   And then bethought him Little Musgrave,
   'This lady's heart have I won.'

5. Quoth she, 'I have loved thee, Little Musgrave,
   Full long and many a day.'—
   'So have I loved you, fair ladye,
   Yet never word durst I say.'—

6. 'But I have a bower at Bucklesfordberry,
      Full daintily it is dight;
   If thou'lt wend thither, thou Little Musgrave,
      Thou's lig in my arms all night.'

7. Quoth he, 'I thank thee, fair ladye,
      This kindness thou showest to me;
   And whether it be to my weal or woe
      This night I will lodge with thee.'

8. With that beheard a little tiny page,
      By his lady's coach as he ran.
   Says, 'Although I am my lady's foot-page,
      Yet I am Lord Barnard's man.'

9. Then he's cast off his hose and shoon,
      Set down his feet and ran,
   And where the bridges were broken down
      He bent his bow and swam.

10. 'Awake! awake! thou Lord Barnard,
       As thou art a man of life!
    Little Musgrave is at Bucklesfordberry
       Along with thy own wedded wife.'—

11. 'If this be true, thou little tiny page,
       This thing thou tellest to me,
    Then all the land in Bucklesfordberry
       I freely will give to thee.

12. 'But if it be a lie, thou little tiny page,
    This thing thou tellest to me,
  On the highest tree in Bucklesfordberry
    Then hangèd shalt thou be.'

13. He callèd up his merry men all:
    'Come saddle me my steed;
  This night must I to Bucklesfordberry,
    For I never had greater need.'

14. But some they whistled, and some they sung,
    And some they thus could say,
  Whenever Lord Barnard's horn it blew:
    '*Away, Musgrave, away!* . . .

15. 'Methinks I hear the threstle cock,
    Methinks I hear the jay;
  Methinks I hear Lord Barnard's horn,
    Away, Musgrave, away!'—

16. 'Lie still, lie still, thou little Musgrave,
    And huggle me from the cold;
  'Tis nothing but a shepherd's boy
    A-driving his sheep to the fold.'

17. By this, Lord Barnard came to his door
    And lighted a stone upon;
  And he's pull'd out three silver keys,
    And open'd the doors each one.

18. He lifted up the coverlet,
    He lifted up the sheet;
  'Dost thou like my bed, Little Musgrave?
    Dost thou find my lady sweet?'—

19. 'I find her sweet,' quoth Little Musgrave,
    'The more 'tis to my pain;
  I would gladly give three hundred pounds
    That I were on yonder plain.'—

20. 'Arise, arise, thou Little Musgrave,
    And put thy clothès on;
  It shall ne'er be said in my country
    I have kill'd a naked man.

21. 'I have two swords in one scabbard,
    They are both sharp and clear;
  Take you the best, and I the worst,
    We'll end the matter here.'

22. The first stroke Little Musgrave struck,
    He hurt Lord Barnard sore;
  The next stroke that Lord Barnard struck,
    Little Musgrave ne'er struck more.

23. With that bespake this fair lady,
    In bed where as she lay:
  'Although thou'rt dead, thou Little Musgrave
    Yet I for thee will pray.

24. 'And wish well to thy soul will I
    So long as I have life;
    So will I not for thee, Barnard,
    Although I'm thy wedded wife.'

25. He cut her paps from off her breast;
    Great pity it was to see
    That some drops of this lady's heart's blood
    Ran trickling down her knee.

26. 'Woe worth you, woe worth, my merry men all,
    You were ne'er born for my good!
    Why did you not offer to stay my hand
    When you saw me wax so wood?

27. 'For I have slain the fairest lady
    That ever wore woman's weed,
    Soe I have slain the fairest lady
    That ever did woman's deed.

28. 'A grave, a grave,' Lord Barnard cried,
    'To put these lovers in!
    But lay my lady on the upper hand,
    For she comes of the nobler kin.'

LORD INGRAM AND CHILDE VYET

1. Lord Ingram and Childe Vyet
   Were both born in one hall;
   Laid both their hearts on one lady;
   The worse did them befall.

2. Lord Ingram woo'd Lady Maisry
   From father and from mother;
   Lord Ingram woo'd Lady Maisry
   From sister and from brother;

3. Lord Ingram woo'd Lady Maisry
   With leave of all her kin;
   And every one gave full consent,
   But she said 'no' to him.

4. Now it fell out, upon a day
   She was dressing of her head,
   That in did come her father dear,
   Wearing the gold so red.

5. 'Get up now, Lady Maisry,
   Put on your wedding-gown;
   For Lord Ingram he will be here,
   Your wedding must be done.'—

6. 'I'd rather be Childe Vyet's wife,
   The white fish for to sell,
   Before I were Lord Ingram's wife,
   To wear the silk so well.

7. 'I'd rather be Childe Vyet's wife,
   With him to beg my bread,
   Before I were Lord Ingram's wife,
   To wear the gold so red. . . .

8. 'O where will I get a bonny boy,
   Will win gold to his fee,
And will run unto Childe Vyet
   With this letter from me?'—

9. 'O here I am, the boy,' says one,
   'Will win gold to my fee,
And carry away any letter
   To Childe Vyet from thee.'

10. The first line that Childe Vyet read,
   A grievèd man was he;
The next line that Childe Vyet read,
   A tear blinded his e'e.
'I wonder what ails my one brother,
   He'll not let my love be!

11. 'But I'll send to my brother's bridal —
   The gammons o' the swine —
With four and twenty buck and roe,
   And ten tun of the wine;
And bid my love be blithe and glad,
   And I will follow syne.'

12. There was no groom in that castle
   But got a gown of green;
And all was blithe, and all was glad,
   But Lady Maisry was neen.

13. There was no cook in that kitchen
    But got a gown of grey;
  And all was blithe, and all was glad,
    But Lady Maisry was wae.

14. O sweetly play'd the merry organs
    Within her mother's bower;
  But dumb stood Lady Maisry,
    And let the tears down pour.

15. O sweetly play'd the harp so fine
    Within her father's hall;
  But still stood Lady Maisry,
    And let the tears down fall.

16. 'Tween Mary Kirk and the castle
    Was all spread o'er with garl,
  To keep Lady Maisry and her maidens
    From tramping on the marl.

17. From Mary Kirk to the castle
    Was spread a cloth of gold,
  To keep Lady Maisry and her maidens
    From treading upon the mould.

18. When mass was sung, and bells were rung
    And all men bound for bed,
  Lord Ingram and Lady Maisry
    In one bed they were laid.

19. When they were laid into one bed,
    It was both soft and warm;
  He laid his hand over her side,
    Says, 'I think you are with bairn.'—

20. 'I told you once, so did I twice,
    When ye came for my wooer,
  That Childe Vyet, your one brother,
    One night lay in my bower.

21. ' I told you twice, I told you thrice,
    Ere ye came me to wed,
  That Childe Vyet, your one brother,
    One night lay in my bed.'—

22. 'O father your bairn on me, Maisry,
    And on no other man;
  And I'll gie him to his dowry
    Full fifty ploughs of land.'—

23. 'I will not father my bairn on you,
    Nor on no wrongeous man,
  Though ye'd give him to his dowry
    Five thousand ploughs of land.'

24. He has taken out his trusty sword
    And laid it between them tway;
  Says, 'Lie you there, you ill woman,
    A maid for me till day.'

25. Then in it came him Childe Vyet,
    Shed back his yellow hair,
    And gave Lord Ingram to the heart
    A deep wound and a sair.

26. Then up did start him Lord Ingram
    Shed back his coal-black hair,
    And gave Childe Vyet to the heart
    A deep wound and a sair.

27. There was no pity for those two lords,
    In bower where they lay slain;
    But all was for Lady Maisry,
    In bower where she went brain.

28. Says, 'If I have been an ill woman,
    Alas, and woe is me!
    And if I have been an ill woman,
    A good woman I'll be.

29. 'Ye'll take from me my silk attire,
    Bring me a palmer's weed;
    And for their sakes the world thoro'
    I'll gang and beg my bread.

30. 'If I gang a step for Childe Vyet,
    For Lord Ingram I'll gang three;
    All for the honour that he paid
    At Mary Kirk to me.'

FAIR JANET

1. 'YE maun gang to your father, Janet,
      Ye maun gang to him sune;
   Ye maun gang to your father, Janet,
      In case that his days are dune.'

2. Janet's awa' to her father
      As fast as she could hie:
   'O what's your will wi' me, father?
      O what's your will wi' me?'—

3. 'My will wi' you, Fair Janet,' he said,
      . 'It is both bed and board;
   Some say that ye love Sweet Willie,
      But ye maun wed a French lord.'

4. Janet's awa to her chamber
      As fast as she could go;
   Wha's the first ane that tappèd there,
      But Sweet Willie her jo?

5. 'O we maun part this love, Willie,
      That has been lang between;
   There's a French lord coming o'er the sea
      To wed me wi' a ring.'—

6. 'If we maun part this love, Janet,
      It causeth mickle woe;
   If we maun part this love, Janet,
      It makes me in mourning go.'—

7. 'But ye maun gang to your three sisters,
      Meg, Marion and Jean;
   Tell them to come to Fair Janet,
      In case that her days are dune.'

8. Willie's awa' to his three sisters,
      Meg, Marion and Jean:
   'O haste and gang to Fair Janet,
      I fear that her days are dune!'

9. Some drew to them their silken hose,
      Some drew to them their shoon,
   Some drew to them their silk manteils,
      Their coverings to put on;
   And they're awa' to Fair Janet
      By the hie light o' the moon. . . .

10. 'O I have borne this babe, Willie,
      Wi' mickle toil and pain;
   Take hame, take hame your babe, Willie,
      For nurse I dare be nane.'

11. He's ta'en his young son in his arms
      And kiss'd him cheek and chin,
   And he's awa' to his mother's bower
      By the hie light o' the moon.

12. 'O open, open, mother!' he says,
      'O open, and let me in!
   The rain rains on my yellow hair
      And the dew drops o'er my chin;

And I hae my young son in my arms,—
    I fear that his days are dune.'

13. Then with her fingers long and sma'
    She lifted up the pin,
  And with her arms sae long and sma'
    Received the baby in.

14. 'Gae back, gae back now, Sweet Willie,
    And comfort your fair ladye;
  For where ye had but ae nourice
    Your young son shall hae three.'

15. Willie he was scarce awa'
    And Janet put to bed,
  When in and came her father dear:
    'Mak' haste, and busk the bride!'—

16. 'There's a sair pain in my head, father,
    There's a sair pain in my side;
  And ill, O ill I am, father,
    This day for to be a bride!'—

17. 'O ye maun busk this bonny bride,
    And put a gay mantle on;
  For she shall wed this auld French lord,
    Gin she should die this morn.'

18. Some put on the gay green robes,
    And some put on the brown;
  But Janet put on the scarlet robes,
    Shone foremost thro' the town.

19. And some they mounted the black steed,
    And some mounted the brown;
    But Janet mounted the milk-white steed,
    Rode foremost thro' the town.

20. 'O wha will guide your horse, Janet?
    O wha will guide him best?'—
    'O wha but Willie, my true-love?
    He kens I love him best.'

21. And when they came to Mary's kirk
    To tie the holy ban',
    Fair Janet's colour gaed and came,
    And her cheek look'd pale and wan.

22. When dinner it was past and done,
    And dancing to begin,
    'O we'll go take the bride's maidens,
    And we'll go fill the ring.'

23. O ben then came the auld French lord,
    Saying, 'Bride, will ye dance wi' me?'—
    'Awa', awa', ye auld French lord!
    Your face I downa see.'

24. O ben then came Sweet Willie,
    He came with ane advance:
    'O I'll go tak' the bride's maidens,
    And we'll go tak' a dance.'—

25. 'I've seen ither days wi' you, Willie,
  And so has mony mae,
 Ye would hae danced wi' me mysel',
  Let a' my maidens gae.'

26. O ben now came Sweet Willie,
  Saying, 'Bride, will ye dance wi' me?'—
 'Ay, by my sooth, and that I will
  Gin my back should break in three.'

27. She hadna danced her o'er the floor,
  She hadna turn'd but thrice,
 When she fell doun at Willie's feet,
  And up did never rise.

28. Willie's ta'en the key of his coffer
  And gi'en it to his man:
 'Gae hame, and tell my mother dear
  My horse he has me slain;
 And bid her be kind to my young son,
  For father he has nane.'

LORD THOMAS AND FAIR ANNET

1. LORD THOMAS and Fair Annet
  Sat all day on a hill;
 When night was come, and sun was set,
  They had not talk'd their fill.

2. Lord Thomas said a word in jest,
  Fair Annet took it ill:
'I'll never wed a tocherless maid
  Against my ain friends' will.'—

3. 'Gif ye'll not wed a tocherless wife,
  A wife will ne'er wed ye:
Fare ye well now, Lord Thomas,
  It's fare ye well a wee.'

4. O Annet she's gane till her bower,
  Lord Thomas down the den;
And he's come till his mither's bower
  By the lee light o' the moon.

5. 'O sleep ye, wake ye, mither?' he says,
  'Or are ye the bower within?'—
'I sleep right aft, I wake right aft;
  What want ye with me, son?

6. 'Where have ye been a' night, Thomas?
  O wow, ye've tarried long!'—
'I have been courtin' Fair Annet
  And she is frae me gone

7. 'O rede, O rede, mither,' he says,
  'A gude rede gie to me:
O sall I tak' the nut-brown bride,
  And let Fair Annet be?'—

8. 'The nut-brown bride has gold and gear,
    Fair Annet she's got nane;
  And the little beauty Fair Annet has,
    O it will soon be gane.

9. 'It's an' ye wed the nut-brown bride,
    I'll heap gold wi' my hand;
  But an' ye wed her, Fair Annet,
    I'll straik it wi' a wand.

10. 'The nut-brown bride has sheep and kye,
    Fair Annet she's got nane;
  Son Thomas, for my benison
    Bring ye the brown bride hame.'—

11. 'But alas, alas!' says Lord Thomas,
    'O fair is Annet's face!'—
  'But what matter for that, son Thomas?
    She has nae ither grace.'—

12. 'Alas, alas!' says Lord Thomas,
    'But white is Annet's hand!'—
  'What matter for that, son Thomas?
    She has not a fur' o' land.'—

13. 'Sheep will die in cots, mither,
    And owsen die in byre;
  And what is warldis wealth to me,
    An' I getna my heart's desire?'

14. And he has till his sister gane:
     'Now, sister, rede ye me;
   O sall I marry the nut-brown bride
     And set Fair Annet free?'—

15. 'I'se rede ye tak' Fair Annet, Thomas,
     And let the brown bride alane,
   Lest ye should sign and say Alas!
     What is this we brought hame?'—

16 'No, I will tak' my mither's counsel,
     And marry me out of hand;
   And I will tak' the nut-brown bride;
     Fair Annet may leave the land.'

17. Up then rose Fair Annet's father
     Twa hours or it were day,
   And he is gone to Fair Annet,
     To the bower wherein she lay.

18. 'Rise up, rise up, Fair Annet,' he says,
     'Put on your silken sheen;
   Ye are bidden come to St. Mary's Kirk,
     To see a rich weddin'.'. . .

19. 'My maids, gae to my dressing-room
     And dress to me my hair;
   Where'er ye laid a plait before
     See ye lay ten times mair.

20. 'My maids gae to my dressing-room
  And dress to me my smock;
The one half is o' the holland fine,
  The other o' needle-work.'

21. At yae tett o' her horse's mane
  Was tied a silver bell,
And yae tift o' the norland wind
  It gar'd them a' to knell.

22. Four and twenty gay good knights
  Rade by Fair Annet's side,
And four and twenty fair ladies
  As gin she had been a bride.

23. And when she came to Mary's Kirk,
  She shimmer'd like the sun;
The belt that was about her waist
  Was a' wi' pearls bedone.

24. And when she came to Mary's Kirk,
  And sat down in the deas,
The cleiding the Fair Annet had on
  Enlighten'd a' that place.

25. She sat her by the nut-brown bride,
  And her e'en they were sae clear,
Lord Thomas he clean forgat the bride
  When Fair Annet drew near.

26. He had a rose into his hand,
    He gave it kisses three,
  And reaching by the nut-brown bride,
    Laid it on Annet's knee.

27. 'O wha is this, my father dear,
    Blinks in Lord Thomas's e'e?'—
  'O this Lord Thomas's first true-love
    Before he lovèd thee.'

28. Up then spake the nut-brown bride —
    She spake wi' mickle spite:
  'And where gat ye the rose-water
    That washes thy face so white?'—

29. 'O I did get my rose-water
    Where ye will ne'er get nane,
  For I did get that very rose-water
    Into my mither's wame.'

30. The bride she drew a long bodkin
    Frae out her gay head-gear,
  And strake Fair Annet to the heart,
    That word spak' never mair.

31. 'O Christ thee save!' Lord Thomas he said,
    'Methinks thou look'st wondrous wan;
  Thou was used to look with as fresh a colour
    As ever the sun shined on.'

32. 'O art thou blind, Lord Thomas?' she said,
    'Or canst thou not very well see?
  Or dost thou not see my own heart's blood
    Runs trickling down my knee?'

33. Lord Thomas he saw Fair Annet was pale,
    And marvellèd what mote be;
  But when he saw her dear heart's blood,
    All wood-wroth waxèd he.

34. He drew his dagger frae his side,
    That was so sharp and meet,
  And drave it into the nut-brown bride,
    That fell dead at his feet.

35. 'Now stay for me, dear Annet,' he said,
    'Now stay, my dear!' he cried;
  Then strake the dagger untill his heart,
    And fell dead by her side.

BABYLON; OR, THE BONNIE BANKS O' FORDIE

1. THERE were three ladies lived in a bower —
    Eh, wow, bonnie!
  And they went out to pull a flower
    On the bonnie banks o' Fordie.

2. They hadna pu'ed a flower but ane,
  When up started to them a banisht man.

3. He's ta'en the first sister by her hand,
   And he's turn'd her round and made her stand.

4. 'It's whether will ye be a rank robber's wife,
   Or will ye die by my wee pen-knife?'

5. 'It's I'll not be a rank robber's wife,
   But I'll rather die by your wee pen-knife.'

6. He's killed this may, and he's laid her by
   For to bear the red rose company.

7. He's ta'en the second ane by the hand,
   And he's turn'd her round and made her stand.

8. 'It's whether will ye be a rank robber's wife,
   Or will ye die by my wee pen-knife?'

9. 'It's I'll not be a rank robber's wife,
   But I'll rather die by your wee pen-knife.'

10. He's killed this may, and he's laid her by,
    For to bear the red rose company.

11. He's taken the youngest ane by the hand,
    And he's turn'd her round and made her stand.

12. Says, 'Will ye be a rank robber's wife,
    Or will ye die by my wee pen-knife?'

13. 'It's I'll not be a rank robber's wife,
    Nor will I die by your wee pen-knife.

14. 'For in this wood a brother I hae;
    And gin ye kill me, it's he'll kill thee.'

15. 'What's thy brother's name? come tell to me.'
    'My brother's name is Baby Lon.'

16. 'O sister, sister, what have I done!
    O have I done this ill to thee!

17. 'O since I've done this evil deed,
    Good sall never be my meed.'

18. He's taken out his wee pen-knife,
    Eh, wow, bonnie!
  And he's twyn'd himsel' o' his ain sweet life
    On the bonnie banks o' Fordie.

THE GAY GOSHAWK

1. 'O WELL'S me o' my gay goss-hawk,
    That he can speak and flee!
  He'll carry a letter to my love
    Bring back another to me.'—

2. 'O how can I your true-love ken,
    Or how can I her know?
  Whan frae her mouth I never heard couth,
    Nor wi' my eyes her saw.'—

3. 'O well sall ye my true-love ken,
     As soon as you her see;
   For, of a' the flow'rs in fair England,
     The fairest flow'r is she.

4. 'At even at my love's bower-door
     There grows a bowing birk,
   An' sit ye down and sing thereon,
     As she gangs to the kirk.

5. 'An' four-and-twenty ladies fair
     Will wash and go to kirk,
   But well shall ye my true-love ken,
     For she wears gowd on her skirt.

6. 'An' four-and-twenty gay ladies
     Will to the mass repair,
   But well sall ye my true-love ken,
     For she wears gowd on her hair.'

7. O even at that lady's bower-door
     There grows a bowing birk,
   An' he set down and sang thereon,
     As she gaed to the kirk.

8. 'O eet and drink, my marys a',
     The wine flows you among,
   Till I gang to my shot-window,
     An' hear yon bonny bird's song.

9. 'Sing on, sing on, my bonny bird,
    The song ye sang the streen,
For I ken by your sweet singin'
    You're frae my true-love sen.'

10. O first he sang a merry song,
    An' then he sang a grave,
An' then he peck'd his feathers gray,
    To her the letter gave.

11. 'Ha, there's a letter frae your love,
    He says he sent you three;
He canna wait your luve langer,
    But for your sake he'll dee.

12. 'He bids you write a letter to him;
    He says he's sent you five;
He canna wait your luve langer,
    Tho' you're the fairest alive.'—

13. 'Ye bid him bake his bridal-bread,
    And brew his bridal-ale,
An' I'll meet him in fair Scotland
    Lang, lang or it be stale.'

14. She's doen her to her father dear
    Fa'n low down on her knee:
'A boon, a boon, my father dear
    I pray you, grant it me!'—

15. 'Ask on, ask on, my daughter,
    An' granted it sall be;
    Except ae squire in fair Scotland,
    An' him you sall never see.'—

16. 'The only boon, my father dear,
    That I do crave of thee,
    Is, gin I die in southin lands,
    In Scotland to bury me.

17. 'An' the firstin kirk that ye come till,
    Ye gar the bells be rung,
    An' the nextin kirk that ye come till,
    Ye gar the mass be sung.

18. 'An' the thirdin kirk that ye come till,
    You deal gold for my sake,
    An' the fourthin kirk that ye come till,
    You tarry there till night.'

19. She is doen her to her bigly bow'r,
    As fast as she could fare,
    An' she has tane a sleepy draught,
    That she had mixt wi' care.

20. She's laid her down upon her bed,
    An' soon she's fa'n asleep,
    And soon o'er every tender limb
    Cauld death began to creep.

21. Whan night was flown, an' day was come,
      Nae ane that did her see
    But thought she was as surely dead
      As ony lady cou'd be.

22. Her father an' her brothers dear
      Gar'd make to her a bier;
    The tae half was o' guid red gold,
      The tither o' silver clear.

23. Her mither an' her sisters fair
      Gar'd work for her a sark;
    The tae half was o' cambrick fine,
      The tither o' needle wark.

24. The firstin kirk that they came till,
      They gar'd the bells be rung,
    An' the nextin kirk that they came till,
      They gar'd the mass be sung.

25. The thirdin kirk that they came till,
      They dealt gold for her sake,
    An' the fourthin kirk that they came till,
      Lo, there they met her make!

26. 'Lay down, lay down the bigly bier,
      Lat me the dead look on!'—
    Wi' cherry cheeks and ruby lips
      She lay and smil'd on him.

27. 'O ae sheave o' your bread, true-love,
  An' ae glass o' your wine!
 For I hae fasted for your sake
  These fully days is nine.

28. 'Gang hame,gang hame,my seven bold
   brothers,
  Gang hame and sound your horn;
 An' ye may boast in southin lands
  Your sister's play'd you scorn!'

WILLIE'S LYKE-WAKE

1. 'WILLIE, Willie, what makes you sae sad?'
  And the sun shines over the valleys and a' —
 'I lie sairly sick for the love of a maid.'
  Amang the blue flowers and the yellow and a'.

2. 'O Willie, my son, I'll learn you a wile,
 How this pretty fair maid ye may beguile

3. 'Ye maun lie doun just as ye were dead,
 And tak' your windin'-sheet round your head.

4. 'Ye maun gie the bellman his bell-groat,
 To ring your dead-bell at your lover's yett.'

5. Willie lay doun just as he war dead,
 And took his windin'-sheet round his head.

6. He gied the bellman his bell-groat
   To ring his dead-bell at his lover's yett.

7. 'O wha is this that is dead, I hear?'—
   'O wha but Willie that lo'ed ye sae dear?'

8. She is hame to her father's ain bour:
   'I'll gang to yon lyke-wake ae single hour.'—

9. 'Ye maun tak' with you your brither John;
   It's not meet for maidens to venture alone.'—

10. 'I'll not tak' with me my brither John,
    But I'll gang along myself all alone.'

11. It's when she cam' to her true lover's yett,
    She dealt the red gold round for his sak'.

12. It's when she came to her true lover's bed
    She lifted the sheet to look at the dead.

13. He's ta'en her hand sae meek and sae sma',
    And ca'd her his wife before them a'.

14. 'Fair maid, ye cam' without horse or boy,
    But I'll send you home with a merry convoy.'

FAIR MARGARET AND SWEET WILLIAM

1. As it fell out on a long summer's day,
   Two lovers they sat on a hill:
   They sat together that long summer's day,
   And could not talk their fill.

2. 'I see no harm by you, Margaret,
   Nor you see none by me;
   Before to-morrow eight o'clock
   A rich wedding shall you see.'

3. Fair Margaret sat in her bower-window
   Combing her yellow hair,
   She saw Sweet William and his brown bride
   Unto the church draw near.

4. Then down she laid her ivory comb,
   And up she bound her hair;
   She went out from her bower alive
   But alive never more came there.

5. When day was gone, and night was come,
   And all men fast asleep,
   Came in the ghost of fair Margaret,
   And stood at William's feet.

6. 'How like ye the lady, Sweet William,
   That lies in your arms asleep?
   God give you joy of your gay bride-bed,
   And me of my winding-sheet!'

7. When night was gone, and day was come
   And all men waked from sleep,
   His lady said to Sweet William,
   'My dear, I have cause to weep:

8. 'I dream'd a dream, Sweet William,
   That seldom comes to good:
   My bower was fill'd with wild-wood swine,
   And our bride-bed full of blood.'

9. He callèd up his merry men all,
   By one, by two, by three,
   Saying, 'I'll away to Fair Margaret's bower,
   With the leave of my ladye.'

10. And when he came to Fair Margaret's bower
    He knockèd at the ring;
    And who so ready as her seven brothers
    To rise and let him in?

11. 'O, is she in the parlour?' he said,
    'Or is she in the hall?
    Or is she in the long chamber
    Amongst her merry maids all?'—

12. 'No, she's not in the parlour,' they said,
    'Nor she's not in the hall:
    But she is in the long chamber,
    Laid out against the wall.'—

13. He turnèd up the covering-sheet,
    And look'd upon the dead.
  'Methinks her lips are pale and wan,
    She has lost her cherry red.'

14. With that bespake the seven brothers,
    Making a piteous moan:
  'You may go kiss your jolly brown bride,
    And let our sister alone.'—

15. 'If I do kiss my jolly brown bride,
    I do but what is right;
  For I made no vow to your sister dear,
    By day nor yet by night.

16. 'Deal on, deal on, my merry men all,
    Deal on your cake and wine!
  For whatever is dealt at her funeral to-day
    Shall be dealt to-morrow at mine.'

17. Fair Margaret died on the over night,
    Sweet William died on the morrow:
  Fair Margaret died for pure, pure love,
    Sweet William died for sorrow.

18. Go with your right to Newcastle,
    And come with your left side home;
  There you will see these two lovers
    Lie printed on one stone.

THE TWA BROTHERS

1. THERE were twa brethren in the North,
     They went to school thegither;
   The one unto the other said,
     'Will you try a warsle, brither?'

2. They warsled up, they warsled down,
     Till Sir John fell to the ground,
   And there was a knife in Sir Willie's pouch
     Gied him a deadly wound.

3. 'Tak' aff, tak' aff my holland sark,
     Rive it frae gare to gare,
   And stap it in my bleeding wound —
     'Twill aiblins bleed nae mair.'

4. He's pu'it aff his holland sark,
     Rave it frae gare to gare,
   And stapt it in his bleeding wound —
     But aye it bled the mair.

5. 'O tak' now aff my green cleiding
     And row me saftly in.
   And carry me up to Chester kirk,
     Whar the grass grows fair and green.

6. 'But what will ye say to your father dear
     When ye gae home at e'en?'—
   'I'll say ye're lying at Chester kirk,
     Whar the grass grows fair and green.'—

7. 'O no, O no, when he speers for me
   Saying, "William, whar is John?"
   Ye'll say ye left me at Chester school
   Leaving the school alone.'

8. He's ta'en him up upo' his back,
   And borne him hence away,
   And carried him to Chester kirk,
   And laid him in the clay.

9. But when he sat in his father's chair,
   He grew baith pale and wan:
   'O what blude's that upon your brow?
   And whar is your brither John?'—

10. 'O John's awa' to Chester school,
    A scholar he'll return;
    He bade me tell his father dear
    About him no' to mourn.

11. 'And it is the blude o' my gude grey steed;
    He wadna hunt for me.'—
    'O thy steed's blude was ne'er so red,
    Nor ne'er so dear to me!

12. 'And whaten blude's that upon your dirk?
    Dear Willie, tell to me.'—
    'It is the blude o' my ae brither
    And dule and wae is me!'—

13. 'O what sall I say to your mither?
    Dear Willie, tell to me.'—
    'I'll saddle my steed and awa' I'll ride,
    To dwell in some far countrie.'—

14. 'O when will ye come hame again?
    Dear Willie, tell to me!'—
    'When the sun and moon dance on yon green:
    And that will never be!'

THE CRUEL BROTHER

1. THERE were three ladies play'd at the ba',
    With a hey ho! and a lily gay!
   By came a knight and he woo'd them a'
    As the primrose spreads so sweetly.
      Sing Annet, and Marret, and fair Maisrie,
      As the dew hangs i' the wood, gay ladie!

2. The first ane she was clad in red:
   'O lady fair, Will you be my bride?'

3. The midmost ane was clad in green:
   'O lady fair, will you be my queen?'

4. The youngest o' them was clad in white:
   'O lady fair, be my heart's delight!'—

5. 'Sir knight, ere ye my favour win,
   Ye maun get consent frae a' my kin.

6. 'Ye maun go ask my father, the King:
   Sae maun ye ask my mither, the Queen.

7. 'Sae maun ye ask my sister Anne,
   And dinna forget my brother John.'

8. He has sought her from her father, the King:
   And sae did he her mither, the Queen.

9. He has sought her from her sister Anne:
   But he has forgot her brither John.

10. Now when the wedding day was come,
    The knight would take his bonny bride home.

11. And many a lord and many a knight
    Came to behold that ladie bright.

12. And there was nae man that did her see
    But wish'd himself bridegroom to be.

13. Her father led her down the stair,
    And her mither dear she kiss'd her there.

14. Her sister Anne led her thro' the close,
    And her brither John set her on her horse.

15. She lean'd her o'er the saddle-bow,
    To give him a kiss ere she did go.

16. He has ta'en a knife, baith lang and sharp,
    And stabb'd that bonny bride to the heart.

17. She hadna ridden half thro' the town,
    Until her heart's blude stain'd her gown.

18. 'Ride saftly up,' said the best young man;
    'I think our bride come hooly on.'

19. 'Ride up, ride up,' said the second man;
    'I think our bride looks pale and wan.'

20. Up then comes the gay bridegroom,
    And straight unto the bride he came.

21. 'Does your side-saddle sit awry?
    Or does your steed go heavily?'—

22. 'O lead me gently over yon stile,
    For there would I sit and bleed awhile.

23. 'O lead me gently up yon hill,
    For there would I sit and make my will.'—

24. 'O what will you leave to your father dear?'—
    'The milk-white steed that brought me here.'–

25. 'What will you leave to your mother dear?'—
    'My wedding shift that I do wear.'—

26. 'What will you leave to your sister Anne?'—
    'My silken snood and my golden fan.'—

27. 'What will you leave to your brither John?'—
    With a hay ho! and a lily gay!

'The gallows-tree to hang him on.'
And the primrose spreads so sweetly.
Sing Annet, and Marret, and fair Maisrie,
And the dew hangs i' the wood, gay ladie!

EDWARD, EDWARD

1. 'WHY does your brand sae drop wi' blude,
        Edward, Edward?
   Why does your brand sae drop wi' blude,
        And why sae sad gang ye, O?'—
   'O I hae kill'd my hawk sae gude,
        Mither, mither;
   O I hae kill'd my hawk sae gude,
        And I had nae mair but he, O.'   .

2. 'Your hawk's blude was never sae red,
        Edward, Edward;
   Your hawk's blude was never sae red,
        My dear son, I tell thee, O.'—
   'O I hae kill'd my red-roan steed,
        Mither, mither;
   O I hae kill'd my red-roan steed,
        That erst was sae fair and free, O.'

3. 'Your steed was auld, and ye hae got mair,
        Edward, Edward;
   Your steed was auld, and ye hae got mair;
        Some other dule ye dree, O.'—

'O I hae kill'd my father dear,
  Mither, mither;
O I hae kill'd my father dear,
  Alas, and wae is me, O!'

4. 'And whatten penance will ye dree for that,
    Edward, Edward?
  Whatten penance will ye dree for that?
    My dear son, now tell me, O.'—
  'I'll set my feet in yonder boat,
    Mither, mither;
  I'll set my feet in yonder boat,
    And I'll fare over the sea, O.'

5. 'And what will ye do wi' your tow'rs and your
    ha',
      Edward, Edward?
  And what will ye do wi' your tow'rs and your
    ha',
      That were sae fair to see, O?'—
  'I'll let them stand till they doun fa',
    Mither, mither;
  I'll let them stand till they doun fa',
    For here never mair maun I be, O.'

6. 'And what will ye leave to your bairns and your
    wife,
      Edward, Edward?
  And what will ye leave to your bairns and your
    wife,
      When ye gang owre the sea, O?'—

'The warld's room: let them beg through life,
  Mither, mither;
The warld's room: let them beg through life;
  For them never mair will I see, O.'

7. 'And what will ye leave to your ain mither dear,
    Edward, Edward?
  And what will ye leave to your ain mither dear,
    My dear son, now tell me, O?'—
  'The curse of hell frae me sall ye bear,
    Mither, mither;
  The curse of hell frae me sall ye bear:
    Sic counsels ye gave to me, O!'

LORD RANDAL

1. 'O WHERE hae ye been, Lord Randal, my son?
  O where hae ye been, my handsome young man?'—
  'I hae been to the wild wood; mother, make my
    bed soon,
  For I'm weary wi' hunting, and fain wald lie
    down.

2. 'Where gat ye your dinner, Lord Randal, my son?
  Where gat ye your dinner, my handsome young
    man?'—
  'I dined wi' my true-love; mother, make my bed
    soon,

For I'm weary wi' hunting, and fain wald lie
   down.'

3. 'What gat ye to your dinner, Lord Randal, my
       son?
   What gat ye to your dinner, my handsome young
       man?'—
   'I gat eels boil'd in broo'; mother, make my bed
       soon,
   For I'm weary wi' hunting, and fain wald lie
       down.'

4. 'What became of your bloodhounds, Lord Ran-
       dal, my son?
   What became of your bloodhounds, my hand-
       some young man?'—
   'O they swell'd and they died; mother, make my
       bed soon,
   For I'm weary wi' hunting, and fain wald lie
       down.'

5. 'O I fear ye are poison'd, Lord Randal, my son!
   O I fear ye are poison'd, my handsome young
       man!'—
   'O yes! I am poison'd; mother, make my bed
       soon,
   For I'm sick at the heart, and I fain wald lie
       down.'

THE TWA CORBIES

(SCOTTISH VERSION)

1. As I was walking all alane,
   I heard twa corbies making a mane:
   The tane unto the tither did say,
   'Whar sall we gang and dine the day?'

2. '— In behint yon auld fail dyke
   I wot there lies a new-slain knight;
   And naebody kens that he lies there
   But his hawk, his hound, and his lady fair.

3. 'His hound is to the hunting gane,
   His hawk to fetch the wild-fowl hame,
   His lady's ta'en anither mate,
   So we may mak' our dinner sweet.

4. 'Ye'll sit on his white hause-bane,
   And I'll pike out his bonny blue e'en:
   Wi' ae lock o' his gowden hair
   We'll theek our nest when it grows bare.

5. 'Mony a one for him maks mane,
   But nane sall ken whar he is gane:
   O'er his white banes, when they are bare,
   The wind sall blaw for evermair.'

THE THREE RAVENS

1. THERE were three ravens sat on a tree,
   They were as black as they might be.

2. The one of them said to his make,
   'Where shall we our breakfast take?'

3. 'Down in yonder greenè field
   There lies a knight slain under his shield;

4. 'His hounds they lie down at his feet,
   So well do they their master keep;

5. 'His hawks they flie so eagerly,
   There's no fowl dare come him nigh.

6. 'Down there comes a fallow doe
   As great with young as she might goe.

7. 'She lift up his bloudy head
   And kist his wounds that were so red.

8. 'She gat him up upon her back
   And carried him to earthen lake.

9. 'She buried him before the prime,
   She was dead herself ere evensong time.

10. 'God send every gentleman
    Such hounds, such hawks, and such a
    leman!'

BOOK III

THE NUT-BROWN MAID

1. *He.* *Be it right or wrong, these men among*
    On women do complain;
Affirming this, how that it is
    A labour spent in vain
To love them wele; for never a dele
    They love a man again:
For let a man do what he can
    Their favour to attain,
Yet if a new to them pursue,
    Their first true lover than
Laboureth for naught; for from her thought
    He is a banished man.

2. *She.* *I say not nay, but that all day*
    It is both written and said
That woman's faith is, as who saith,
    All utterly decay'd:
But nevertheless, right good witnèss
    In this case might be laid
That they love true and continùe:
    Record the Nut-brown Maid,
Which, when her love came her to prove,
    To her to make his moan,

163

Would not depart; for in her heart
She loved but him alone.

3. *He.* *Then between us let us discuss*
    What was all the manere
Between them two: we will also
    Tell all the pain in fere   .
That she was in. Now I begin,
    So that ye me answere:
Wherefore all ye that present be,
    I pray you, give an ear.
I am the Knight. I come by night,
    As secret as I can,
Saying, Alas! thus standeth the case,
    I am a banished man.

4. *She.* *And I your will for to fulfil*
    In this will not refuse;
Trusting to show, in wordès few,
    That men have an ill use —
To their own shame — women to blame,
    And causeless them accuse.
Therefore to you I answer now,
    All women to excuse:
Mine own heart dear, with you what cheer?
    I pray you, tell anone;
For, in my mind, of all mankind
    I love but you alone.

5. *He.* It standeth so: a deed is do
   Whereof great harm shall grow:
  My destiny is for to die
   A shameful death, I trow;
  Or else to flee. The t' one must be.
   None other way I know
  But to withdraw as an outlàw,
   And take me to my bow.
  Wherefore adieu, mine own heart true!
   None other rede I can:
  For I must to the green-wood go,
   Alone, a banished man.

6. *She.* O Lord, what is this worldis bliss,
   That changeth as the moon!
  My summer's day in lusty May
   Is darked before the noon.
  I hear you say, farewell: Nay, nay,
   ' We dèpart not so soon.
  Why say ye so? whither will ye go?
   Alas! what have ye done?
  All my welfàre to sorrow and care
   Should change, if ye were gone:
  For, in my mind, of all mankind
   I love but you alone.

7. *He.* I can believe it shall you grieve,
   And somewhat you distrain;
  But afterward, your painès hard
   Within a day or twain

Shall soon aslake; and ye shall take
  Comfort to you again.
Why should ye ought? for, to make
    thought,
  Your labour were in vain.
And thus I do; and pray you to,
  As hartèly as I can:
For I must to the green-wood go,
  Alone, a banished man.

8. *She.* Now, sith that ye have showed to me
    The secret of your mind,
  I shall be plain to you again,
    Like as ye shall me find.
  Sith it is so that ye will go,
    I will not live behind.
  Shall never be said the Nut-brown Maid
    Was to her love unkind.
  Make you readỳ, for so am I,
    Although it were anone:
  For, in my mind, of all mankind
    I love but you alone.

9. *He.* Yet I you rede to take good heed
    What men will think and say:
  Of young, of old, it shall be told
    That ye be gone away
  Your wanton will for to fulfil,
    In green-wood you to play;

And that ye might for your delight
  No longer make delay.
Rather than ye should thus for me
  Be called an ill womàn
Yet would I to the green-wood go,
  Alone, a banished man.

10. *She.* Though it be sung of old and young
      That I should be to blame,
    Theirs be the charge that speak so large
      In hurting of my name:
    For I will prove that faithful love
      It is devoid of shame;
    In your distress and heaviness
      To part with you the same:
    And sure all tho that do not so
      True lovers are they none:
    For, in my mind, of all mankind
      I love but you alone.

11. *He.* I counsel you, Remember how
      It is no maiden's law
    Nothing to doubt, but to run out
      To wood with an outlàw.
    For ye must there in your hand bear
      A bow readỳ to draw;
    And as a thief thus must you live
      Ever in dread and awe,

Whereby to you great harm might grow:
  Yet had I liever than
That I had to the green-wood go,
  Alone, a banished man.

12. *She.* I think not nay but as ye say;
  It is no maiden's lore;
But love may make me for your sake,
  As I have said before,
To come on foot, to hunt and shoot,
  To get us meat and store;
For so that I your company
  May have, I ask no more.
From which to part it maketh my heart
  As cold as any stone;
For, in my mind, of all mankind
  I love but you alone.

13. *He.* For an outlàw this is the law,
  That men him take and bind:
Without pitie, hangèd to be,
  And waver with the wind.
If I had need (as God forbede!)
  What socours could ye find?
Forsooth, I trow, you and your bow
  For fear would draw behind.
And no mervail; for little avail
  Were in your counsel than:
Wherefore I'll to the green-wood go,
  Alone, a banished man.

14. *She.* Right well know ye that women be
   But feeble for to fight;
  No womanhede it is, indeed,
   To be bold as a knight:
  Yet in such fear if that ye were
   With enemies day and night,
  I would withstand, with bow in hand,
   To grieve them as I might,
  And you to save; as women have
   From death men many one:
  For, in my mind, of all mankind
   I love but you alone.

15. *He.* Yet take good hede; for ever I drede
   That ye could not sustain
  The thorny ways, the deep vallèys,
   The snow, the frost, the rain,
  The cold, the heat; for dry or wete,
   We must lodge on the plain;
  And, us above, no other roof
   But a brake bush or twain:
  Which soon should grieve you, I believe;
   And ye would gladly than
  That I had to the green-wood go,
   Alone, a banished man.

16. *She.* Sith I have here been partynere
   With you of joy and bliss,
  I must alsò part of your woe
   Endure, as reason is:

Yet I am sure of one pleasùre,
    And shortly it is this —
That where ye be, me seemeth, pardé,
    I could not fare amiss.
Without more speech I you beseech
    That we were shortly gone;
For, in my mind, of all mankind
    I love but you alone.

17. *He.* If ye go thyder, ye must consider,
    When ye have lust to dine,
There shall no meat be for to gete,
    Nether bere, ale, ne wine,
Ne shetès clean, to lie between,
    Made of the thread and twine;
None other house, but leaves and boughs,
    To cover your head and mine.
Lo, mine heart sweet, this ill diète
    Should make you pale and wan:
Wherefore I'll to the green-wood go,
    Alone, a banished man.

18. *She.* Among the wild deer such an archère,
    As men say that ye be,
Ne may not fail of good vitayle
    Where is so great plentè:
And water clear of the rivere
    Shall be full sweet to me;

With which in hele I shall right wele
    Endure, as ye shall see;
And, or we go, a bed or two
    I can provide anone;
For, in my mind, of all mankind
    I love but you alone.

19. *He.* Lo yet, before, ye must do more,
        If ye will go with me:
    As, cut your hair up by your ear,
        Your kirtle by the knee;
    With bow in hand for to withstand
        Your enemies, if need be:
    And this same night, before daylight,
        To woodward will I flee.
    If that ye will all this fulfil,
        Do it shortly as ye can:
    Else will I to the green-wood go,
        Alone, a banished man.

20. *She.* I shall as now do more for you
        Than 'longeth to womanhede;
    To short my hair, a bow to bear,
        To shoot in time of need.
    O my sweet mother! before all other
        For you I have most drede!
    For now, adieu! I must ensue
        Where fortune doth me lead

All this make ye: Now let us flee;
   The day cometh fast upon:
For, in my mind, of all mankind
   I love but you alone.

21. *He.* Nay, nay, not so; ye shall not go,
    And I shall tell you why —
   Your appetite is to be light
    Of love, I well espy:
   For, right as ye have said to me,
    In likewise hardily
   Ye would answere whosoever it were,
    In way of companỳ:
   It is said of old, Soon hot, soon cold;
    And so is a womàn:
   Wherefore I to the wood will go,
    Alone, a banished man.

22. *She.* If ye take heed, it is no need
    Such words to say to me;
   For oft ye prayed, and long assayed,
    Or I loved you, pardè:
   And though that I of ancestry
    A baron's daughter be,
   Yet have you proved how I you loved,
    A squire of low degree;
   And ever shall, whatso befall,
    To die therefore anone;
   For, in my mind, of all mankind
    I love but you alone.

23. *He.*   A baron's child to be beguiled,
              It were a cursèd deed!
           To be felàw and an outlaw —
              Almighty God forbede!
           Yet better were the poor squyere
              Alone to forest yede
           Than ye shall say another day
              That by my cursèd rede
           Ye were betrayed. Wherefore, good maid,
              The best rede that I can,
           Is, that I to the green-wood go,
              Alone, a banished man.

24. *She.* Whatever befall, I never shall
              Of this thing be upbraid:
           But if ye go, and leave me so,
              Then have ye me betrayed.
           Remember you wele, how that ye dele;
              For if ye, as ye said,
           Be so unkind to leave behind
              Your love, the Nut-brown Maid,
           Trust me trulỳ that I shall die
              Soon after ye be gone:
           For, in my mind, of all mankind
              I love but you alone.

25. *He.*   If that ye went, ye should repent;
              For in the forest now

I have purveyed me of a maid
  Whom I love more than you:
Another more fair than ever ye were
  I dare it well avow;
And of you both each should be wroth
  With other, as I trow:
It were mine ease to live in peace;
  So will I, if I can:
Wherefore I to the wood will go,
  Alone, a banished man.

26. *She.* Though in the wood I understood
       Ye had a paramour,
    All this may nought remove my thought,
       But that I will be your':
    And she shall find me soft and kind
       And courteis every hour;
    Glad to fulfil all that she will
       Command me, to my power:
    For had ye, lo, an hundred mo,
       Yet would I be that one:
    For, in my mind, of all mankind
       I love but you alone.

27. *He.* Mine own dear love, I see the prove
       That ye be kind and true;
    Of maid, of wife, in all my life,
       The best that ever I knew.
    Be merry and glad; be no more sad;
       The case is changèd new;

For it were ruth that for your truth
  Ye should have cause to rue.
Be not dismayed, whatsoever I said
  To you when I began;
I will not to the green-wood go;
  I am no banished man.

28. *She.* These tidings be more glad to me
    Than to be made a queen,
  If I were sure they should endure;
    But it is often seen
  When men will break promise they speak
    The wordis on the splene.
  Ye shape some wile me to beguile,
    And steal from me, I ween:
  Then were the case worse than it was,
    And I more wo-begone:
  For, in my mind, of all mankind
    I love but you alone.

29. *He.* Ye shall not nede further to drede:
    I will not disparàge
  You (God defend), sith you descend
    Of so great a linàge.
  Now understand: to Westmoreland,
    Which is my heritage,
  I will you bring; and with a ring,
    By way of marriàge

I will you take, and lady make,
　　As shortly as I can:
Thus have you won an Earle's son,
　　And not a banished man.

30.　　*Here may ye see that women be*
　　　　In love meek, kind, and stable;
　　Let never man reprove them than,
　　　　Or call them variable;
　　But rather pray God that we may
　　　　To them be comfortable;
　　Which sometime proveth such as He loveth,
　　　　If they be charitable.
　　For sith men would that women should
　　　　Be meek to them each one;
　　Much more ought they to God obey,
　　　　And serve but Him alone.

BONNY BEE HO'M

1. By Arthur's Dale as late I went
　　I heard a heavy moan;
　I heard a ladie lamenting sair,
　　And ay she cried 'Ohone!

2. 'Ohone, alas! what shall I do,
　　Tormented night and day!
　I never loved a love but ane,
　　And now he's gone away.

3. 'But I will do for my true-love
   What ladies wou'd think sair;
   For seven year shall come and go
   Ere a kaim gang in my hair.

4. 'There shall neither a shoe gang on my foot,
   Nor a kaim gang in my hair,
   Nor e'er a coal nor candle-light
   Shine in my bower nae mair.'

5. She thought her love had been on the sea,
   Fast sailing to Bee Ho'm;
   But he was in a quiet cham'er,
   Hearing his ladie's moan.

6. 'Be husht, be husht, my ladie dear,
   I pray thee mourn not so;
   For I am deep sworn on a book
   To Bee Ho'm for to go.'

7. She has gien him a chain of the beaten gowd
   And a ring with a ruby stone:
   'As lang as this chain your body binds,
   Your blude can never be drawn.

8. 'But gin this ring shou'd fade or fail,
   Or the stone shou'd change its hue,
   Be sure your love is dead and gone,
   Or she has proved untrue.'

9. He had no been at Bonny Bee Ho'm
   A twelve month and a day,
   Till, looking on his gay gowd ring,
   The stone grew dark and gray.

10. 'O ye take my riches to Bee Ho'm,
    And deal them presentlie,
    To the young that canna, the auld that
    maunna,
    And the blind that does not see.

11. 'Fight on, fight on, my merry men all!
    With you I'll fight no more;
    But I will gang to some holy place
    And pray to the King of Glore.'

SIR PATRICK SPENS

1. *The Sailing*

1. THE king sits in Dunfermline town
   Drinking the blude-red wine;
   'O whare will I get a skeely skipper
   To sail this new ship o' mine?'

2. O up and spak an eldern knight,
   Sat at the king's right knee:
   'Sir Patrick Spens is the best sailor
   That ever sail'd the sea.'

3. Our king has written a braid letter,
   And seal'd it with his hand,
   And sent it to Sir Patrick Spens,
   Was walking on the strand.

4. 'To Noroway, to Noroway,
   To Noroway o'er the faem;
   The king's daughter o' Noroway,
   'Tis thou must bring her hame.'

5. The first word that Sir Patrick read
   So loud, loud laugh'd he;
   The neist word that Sir Patrick read
   The tear blinded his e'e.

6. 'O wha is this has done this deed
   And tauld the king o' me,
   To send us out, at this time o' year,
   To sail upon the sea?

7. 'Be it wind, be it weet, be it hail, be it sleet,
   Our ship must sail the faem;
   The king's daughter o' Noroway,
   'Tis we must fetch her hame.'

8. They hoysed their sails on Monenday morn
   Wi' a' the speed they may;
   They hae landed in Noroway
   Upon a Wodensday.

11. *The Return*

9. 'Mak ready, mak ready, my merry men a'!
    Our gude ship sails the morn.'—
  'Now ever alack, my master dear,
    I fear a deadly storm.

10. 'I saw the new moon late yestreen
    Wi' the auld moon in her arm;
  And if we gang to sea, master,
    I fear we'll come to harm.'

11. They hadna sail'd a league, a league,
    A league but barely three,
  When the lift grew dark, and the wind blew
        loud,
    And gurly grew the sea.

12. The ankers brak, and the topmast lap,
    It was sic a deadly storm:
  And the waves cam owre the broken ship
    Till a' her sides were torn.

13. 'O where will I get a gude sailor
    To tak' my helm in hand,
  Till I get up to the tall topmast
    To see if I can spy land?'—

14. 'O here am I, a sailor gude,
    To tak' the helm in hand,

Till you go up to the tall topmast,
But I fear you'll ne'er spy land.'

15. He hadna gane a step, a step,
A step but barely ane,
When a bolt flew out of our goodly ship,
And the saut sea it came in.

16. 'Go fetch a web o' the silken claith,
Another o' the twine,
And wap them into our ship's side,
And let nae the sea come in.'

17. They fetch'd a web o' the silken claith,
Another o' the twine,
And they wapp'd them round that gude
ship's side,
But still the sea came in.

18. O laith, laith were our gude Scots lords
To wet their cork-heel'd shoon;
But lang or a' the play was play'd
They wat their hats aboon.

19. And mony was the feather bed
That flatter'd on the faem;
And mony was the gude lord's son
That never mair cam hame.

20. O lang, lang may the ladies sit,
Wi' their fans into their hand,

Before they see Sir Patrick Spens
   Come sailing to the strand!

21. And lang, lang may the maidens sit
   Wi' their gowd kames in their hair,
A-waiting for their ain dear loves!
   For them they'll see nae mair.

22. Half-owre, half-owre to Aberdour,
   'Tis fifty fathoms deep;
And there lies gude Sir Patrick Spens,
   Wi' the Scots lords at his feet!

EDOM O' GORDON

1. It fell about the Martinmas,
   When the wind blew shrill and cauld,
Said Edom o' Gordon to his men,
   'We maun draw to a hauld.

2. 'And what a hauld sall we draw to,
   My merry men and me?
We will gae to the house o' the Rodes,
   To see that fair ladye.'

3. The lady stood on her castle wa',
   Beheld baith dale and down;
There she was 'ware of a host of men
   Cam' riding towards the town.

4. 'O see ye not, my merry men a',
   O see ye not what I see?
   Methinks I see a host of men;
   I marvel wha they be.'

5. She ween'd it had been her lovely lord,
   As he cam riding hame;
   It was the traitor, Edom o' Gordon,
   Wha reck'd nae sin nor shame.

6. She had nae sooner buskit hersell,
   And putten on her gown,
   But Edom o' Gordon an' his men
   Were round about the town.

7. They had nae sooner supper set,
   Nae sooner said the grace,
   But Edom o' Gordon an' his men
   Were lighted about the place.

8. The lady ran up to her tower-head,
   Sae fast as she could hie,
   To see if by her fair speeches
   She could wi' him agree.

9. 'Come doun to me, ye lady gay,
   Come doun, come doun to me;
   This night sall ye lig within mine arms,
   To-morrow my bride sall be.'—

10. 'I winna come down, ye fals Gordon,
    I winna come down to thee;
    I winna forsake my ain dear lord,
    That is sae far frae me.'—

11. 'Gie owre your house, ye lady fair,
    Gie owre your house to me; ·
    Or I sall brenn yoursel therein,
    But and your babies three.'—

12. 'I winna gie owre, ye fals Gordon,
    To nae sic traitor as yee;
    And if ye brenn my ain dear babes,
    My lord sall mak ye dree.

13. 'Now reach my pistol, Glaud, my man,
    And charge ye weel my gun;
    For, but an I pierce that bluidy butcher,
    My babes, we been undone!'

14. She stood upon her castle wa',
    And let twa bullets flee:
    She miss'd that bluidy butcher's heart,
    And only razed his knee.

15. 'Set fire to the house!' quo' fals Gordon,
    All wud wi' dule and ire:
    'Fals lady, ye sall rue this deid
    As ye brenn in the fire!'—

16. 'Wae worth, wae worth ye, Jock, my man!
　　I paid ye weel your fee;
　Why pu' ye out the grund-wa' stane,
　　Lets in the reek to me?

17. 'And e'en wae worth ye, Jock, my man!
　　I paid ye weel your hire;
　Why pu' ye out the grund-wa' stane,
　　To me lets in the fire?'—

18. 'Ye paid me weel my hire, ladye,
　　Ye paid me weel my fee:
　But now I'm Edom o' Gordon's man,
　　Maun either do or dee.'

19. O then bespake her little son,
　　Sat on the nurse's knee:
　Says, 'Mither dear, gie owre this house,
　　For the reek it smithers me.'—

20. 'I wad gie a' my gowd, my bairn,
　　Sae wad I a' my fee,
　For ae blast o' the western wind,
　　To blaw the reek frae thee.'

21. O then bespake her dochter dear —
　　She was baith jimp and sma':
　'O row me in a pair o' sheets,
　　And tow me owre the wa'!'

22. They row'd her in a pair o' sheets,
    And tow'd her owre the wa';
    But on the point o' Gordon's spear
    She gat a deadly fa'.

23. O bonnie, bonnie was her mouth,
    And cherry were her cheiks,
    And clear, clear was her yellow hair,
    Whereon the red blood dreips.

24. Then wi' his spear he turn'd her owre;
    O gin her face was wane!
    He said, 'Ye are the first that e'er
    I wish'd alive again.'

25. He turn'd her owre and owre again;
    O gin her skin was white!
    'I might hae spared that bonnie face
    To have been some man's delight.

26. 'Busk and boun, my merry men a',
    For ill dooms I do guess;
    I canna look in that bonnie face
    As it lies on the grass.'—

27. 'Wha looks to freits, my master dear,
    It's freits will follow them;
    Let it ne'er be said that Edom o' Gordon
    Was daunted by a dame.'

28. But when the lady saw the fire
    Come flaming owre her head,
  She wept, and kiss'd her children twain,
    Says, 'Bairns, we been but dead.'

29. The Gordon then his bugle blew,
    And said, 'Awa', awa'!
  This house o' the Rodes is a' in a flame;
    I hauld it time to ga'.'

30. And this way lookit her ain dear lord,
    As he cam owre the lea;
  He saw his castle a' in a lowe,
    As far as he could see.

31. Then sair, O sair, his mind misgave,
    And all his heart was wae:
  'Put on, put on, my wighty men,
    Sae fast as ye can gae.

32. 'Put on, put on, my wighty men,
    Sae fast as ye can drie!
  For he that's hindmost o' the thrang
    Sall ne'er get good o' me.'

33. Then some they rade, and some they ran,
    Out-owre the grass and bent;
  But ere the foremost could win up,
    Baith lady and babes were brent

34. And after the Gordon he is gane,
  Sae fast as he might drie;
 And soon i' the Gordon's foul heart's
   blude
 He's wroken his dear ladye.

LAMKIN

1. It's Lamkin was a mason good
  As ever built wi' stane;
 He built Lord Wearie's castle,
  But payment got he nane.

2. 'O pay me, Lord Wearie,
  Come, pay to me my fee.'—
 'I canna pay you, Lamkin,
  For I maun gang o'er the sea.'—

3. 'O pay me now, Lord Wearie,
  Come, pay me out o' hand.'—
 'I canna pay you, Lamkin,
  Unless I sell my land.'—

4. 'O gin ye winna pay me,
  I here sall mak' a vow,
 Before that ye come hame again,
  Ye sall hae cause to rue.'

5. Lord Wearie got a bonny ship,
  To sail the saut sea faem;

Bade his lady weel the castle keep,
    Ay till he should come hame.

6. 'Gae bar the doors,' the lady said,
    'Gae well the windows pin;
And what care I for Lamkin
    Or any of his gang?'

7. But the nourice was a fause limmer
    As e'er hung on a tree;
She laid a plot wi'.Lamkin,
    Whan her lord was o'er the sea.

8. She laid a plot wi' Lamkin,
    When the servants were awa',
Loot him in at a little shot-window,
    And brought him to the ha'.

9. 'O whare's a' the men o' this house,
    That ca' me the Lamkin?'—
'They're at the barn-well thrashing;
    'Twill be lang ere they come in.'—

10. 'And whare's the women o' this house,
    That ca' me the Lamkin?'—
'They're at the far well washing;
    'Twill be lang ere they come in.'—

11. 'And whare's the bairns o' this house,
    That ca' me the Lamkin?'—

'They're at the school reading;
  'Twill be night or they come hame.'—

12. 'O whare's the lady o' this house,
      That ca's me the Lamkin?'—
    'She's up in her bower sewing,
      But we soon can bring her down.'

13. Then Lamkin's tane a sharp knife,
      That hung down by his gare,
    And he has gi'en the bonny babe
      A deep wound and a sair.

14. Then Lamkin he rockèd,
      And the fause nourice sang,
    Till frae ilka bore o' the cradle
      The red blood out sprang.

15. Then out it spak' the lady,
      As she stood on the stair:
    'What ails my bairn, nourice,
      That he's greeting sae sair?

16. 'O still my bairn, nourice,
      O still him wi' the pap!'
    'He winna still, lady,
      For this nor for that.'—

17. 'O still my bairn, nourice,
      O still him wi' the wand!'—

'He winna still, lady,
　　For a' his father's land.'—

18. 'O still my bairn, nourice,
　　　O still him wi' the bell!'—
　　'He winna still, lady,
　　　Till ye come down yoursel'.'—

19. O the firsten step she steppit,
　　　She steppit on a stane;
　　But the neisten step she steppit,
　　　She met him Lamkin.

20. 'O mercy, mercy, Lamkin,
　　　Hae mercy upon me!
　　Though you hae ta'en my young son's
　　　　life,
　　　Ye may let mysel' be.'—

21. 'O sall I kill her, nourice,
　　　Or sall I lat her be?'—
　　'O kill her, kill her, Lamkin,
　　　For she ne'er was good to me.'—

22. 'O scour the bason, nourice,
　　　And mak' it fair and clean,
　　For to keep this lady's heart's blood,
　　　For she's come o' noble kin.'—

23. 'There need nae bason, Lamkin,
　　　Lat it run through the floor;

What better is the heart's blood
O' the rich than o' the poor?'

24. But ere three months were at an end,
    Lord Wearie came again;
    But dowie, dowie was his heart
    When first he came hame.

25. 'O wha's blood is this,' he says,
    'That lies in the cham'er?'—
    'It is your lady's heart's blood;
    'Tis as clear as the lamer.'—

26. 'And wha's blood is this,' he says,
    'That lies in my ha'?'—
    'It is your young son's heart's blood;
    'Tis the clearest ava'.'

27. O sweetly sang the black-bird
    That sat upon the tree;
    But sairer grat Lamkin,
    When he was condemn'd to dee.

28. And bonny sang the mavis
    Out o' the thorny brake;
    But sairer grat the nourice,
    When she was tied to the stake.

HUGH OF LINCOLN

and The Jew's Daughter

1. A' THE boys of merry Lincoln
Were playing at the ba',
And by it came him sweet Sir Hugh,
And he play'd o'er them a'.

2. He kick'd the ba' with his right foot,
And catch'd it wi' his knee,
And thro'-and-thro' the Jew's window
He gar'd the bonny ba' flee.

3. He's doen him to the Jew's castell,
And walk'd it round about;
And there he saw the Jew's daughter
At the window looking out.

4. 'Throw down the ba', ye Jew's daughter,
Throw down the ba' to me!'—
'Never a bit,' says the Jew's daughter,
'Till up to me come ye.'—

5. 'How will I come up? How can I come up?
How can I come up to thee?
I winna come up, I darena come up,
Without my play-feres three.'

6. She's ta'en her to the Jew's garden,
Where the grass grew long and green,

She's pu'd an apple red and white
To wyle the pretty boy in.

7. She's wyled him in through ae dark door,
And sae has she through nine;
She's laid him on a dressing table,
And stickit him like a swine.

8. And first came out the thick, thick blood,
And syne came out the thin,
And syne came out the bonny heart's blood;
There was no more within.

9. She's row'd him in a cake o' lead,
Bade him lie still and sleep;
She's thrown him into Our Lady's draw-well,
Was fifty fathom deep.

10. When bells were rung, and mass was sung,
And a' the bairns came hame,
Then every lady had hame her son,
But Lady Helen had nane.

11. She's ta'en her mantle her about,
Her coffer by the hand,
And she's gone out to seek her son,
And wander'd o'er the land.

12. She's doen her to the Jew's castell
Where a' were fast asleep;

Cries, 'Bonnie Sir Hugh, O pretty Sir Hugh,
 I pray you to me speak!'

13. She near'd Our Lady's deep draw-well,
 And fell down on her knee:
'Where'er ye be, my sweet Sir Hugh,
 I pray you speak to me!'—

14. 'O the lead is wondrous heavy, mother,
 The well is wondrous deep;
The little penknife sticks in my throat,
 And I downa to ye speak.

15. 'Gae hame, gae hame, my mither dear,
 Prepare my winding sheet,
And at the back o' merry Lincoln
 The morn I will you meet.'

16. Now Lady Helen is gane hame,
 Made him a winding sheet,
And at the back o' merry Lincoln
 The dead corpse did her meet.

17. And a' the bells o' merry Lincoln
 Without men's hands were rung;
And a' the books o' merry Lincoln
 Were read without man's tongue;
And never was such a burial
 Sin' Adam's day begun.

THE HEIR OF LINNE

1. THE bonny heir, and the well-faur'd heir,
    The weary heir o' Linne —
 Yonder he stands at his father's yetts,
    And naebody bids him in.

2. 'O see for he gangs, and see for he stands,
    The unthrifty heir o' Linne!
 O see for he stands on the cauld causey,
    And nane bids him come in!'

3. His father and mother were dead him fro',
    And so was the head o' his kin;
 To the cards and dice that he did run,
    Did neither cease nor blin.

4. To drink the wine that was so clear
    With all he would mak' merrye;
 And then bespake him John o' the Scales,
    To the heir of Linne said he:

5. 'How doest thou, thou Lord of Linne
    Doest want or gold or fee?
 Wilt thou not sell thy lands so broad
    To such a good fellow as me?'

6. He told the gold upon the board,
    Wanted never a bare pennye:
 'The gold is thine, the land is mine,
    The heir of Linne I will be.'

7. 'Here's gold enow,' saith the heir of Linne,
   'For me and my companye.'
   He drank the wine that was so clear,
   And with all he made merrye.

8. Within three quarters of a year
   His gold it waxèd thin;
   His merry men were from him gone,
   Bade him, 'To the de'il ye'se gang!'

9. 'Now well-a-day!' said the heir of Linne,
   'I have left not one pennye.
   God be with my father!' he said,
   'On his land he lived merrilye.'

10. His nourice at her window look'd,
    Beholding dale and down,
    And she beheld this distress'd young man
    Come walking to the town.

11. 'O see for he gangs, and see for he stands,
    The weary heir o' Linne!
    O see for he stands on the cauld causey,
    And nane bids him come in!'—

12. 'Sing owre again that sang, nourice,
    The sang ye sung just now.'—
    'I never sung a sang i' my life
    But I would sing owre to you.

13. 'Come here, come here, Willy,' she said,
  'And rest yoursel' wi' me;
  I hae seen you in better days,
   And in jovial companye.'—

14. 'Gie me a sheave o' your bread, nourice,
  And a bottle o' your wine,
  And I will pay it you owre again
   When I am Lord of Linne.'—

15. 'Ye'se get a sheave o' my bread, Willy,
  And a bottle o' my wine;
  But ye'll pay me when the seas gang dry,
   For ye'll ne'er be Lord o' Linne.

16. Then he turn'd him right and round about,
  As will a woman's son,
  And aff he set and bent his way
   And cam' to the house o' Linne.

17. But when he cam' to that castle,
  They were set down to dine;
  A score of nobles there he saw,
   Sat drinking at their wine.

18. Then some bade gie him beef and fish,
  And some but bane and fin,
  And some bade gie him naething at a',
   But let the palmer gang.

19. Then out it speaks him John o' Scales,
    A saucy word spak' he:
 'Put round the cup, give the beggar a sup,
    Let him fare on his way.'

20. Then out it speaks Sir Ned Magnew,
    Ane o' young Willy's kin:
 'This youth was ance a sprightly boy
    As ever lived in Linne.'

21. He turn'd him right and round about,
    As will a woman's son,
 Then minded him on a little wee key
    That his mother left to him.

22. His mother left him this little wee key
    A little before she deed;
 And bade him keep this little wee key
    Till he was in maist need.

23. Then forth he went, these nobles left
    All drinking in the room;
 Wi' walking rod intill his hand
    He walk'd the castle roun':

24. Till that he found a little door,
    And therein slipp'd the key;
 And there he found three chests in fere
    Of the red and the white monie.

25. Back then through the nobles a'
        He went and did not blin,
    Until he cam' where John o' the Scales
        Was seated at the wine.

26. Then out and spake it John o' Scales,
        He spake wi' mock and jeer:
    'I'd gie a seat to the Lord o' Linne
        If sae be that he were here.

27. 'When the lands o' Linne a-selling were
        A' men said they were free;
    I will sell them twenty pound better cheap
        Nor ever I bought of thee.'—

28. 'I tak' ye to witness, nobles a'!'
        — He cast him a God's pennye —
    'I will buy them twenty pound better cheap
        Nor ever he bought of me.'

29. He's done him to the gaming-table,
        For it stood fair and clean;
    And there he's tould as much rich gold
        As free'd the lands o' Linne.

30. He told the gold there over the board,
        Wanted never a broad pennye;
    'The gold is thine, the land is mine,
        Lord o' Linne again I'll be.'

31. 'Well-a-day!' said John o' the Scales' wife,
    'Well-a-day, and woe is me!
Yesterday I was the Lady o' Linne,
    And now I'm a naebodye!'

32. But 'Fare thee well,' said the heir of Linne,
    'Now John o' the Scales!' said he:
'A curse light on me if ever again
    My lands be in jeopardye!'

YOUNG WATERS

1. ABOUT Yule, when the wind blew cule,
    And the round tables began,
O there is come to our King's court
    Mony a well-favor'd man.

2. The Queen luikt owre the castle-wa',
    Beheld baith dale and down,
And there she saw Young Waters
    Come riding to the town.

3. His footmen they did rin before,
    His horsemen rade behind;
Ane mantel of the burning gowd
    Did keip him frae the wind.

4. Gowden-graith'd his horse before,
    And siller-shod behind;

The horse Young Waters rade upon
Was fleeter than the wind.

5. Out then spak' a wylie lord,
   Unto the Queen said he:
   'O tell me wha's the fairest face
   Rides in the company?'—

6. 'I've sene lord, and I've sene laird,
   And knights of high degree,
   Bot a fairer face than Young Waters'
   Mine eyne did never see.'

7. Out then spake the jealous King,
   And an angry man was he:
   'O if he had bin twice as fair,
   You micht have excepted me.'

8. 'You're neither laird nor lord,' she says,
   'But the King that wears the crown;
   There is not a knight in fair Scotland
   But to thee maun bow down.'

9. For a' that she cou'd do or say,
   Appeas'd he wad nae bee,
   But for the words which she had said,
   Young Waters he maun dee.

10. They hae ta'en Young Waters,
    And put fetters to his feet;

They hae ta'en Young Waters, and
    Thrown him in dungeon deep.

11. 'Aft have I ridden thro' Stirling town,
    In the wind but and the weet;
But I neir rade thro' Stirling town
    Wi' fetters at my feet.

12. 'Aft have I ridden thro' Stirling town,
    In the wind but and the rain;
But I neir rade thro' Stirling town
    Neir to return again.'

13. They hae ta'en to the heiding-hill
    His young son in his craddle;
And they hae ta'en to the heiding-hill
    His horse but and his saddle.

14. They hae ta'en to the heiding-hill
    His lady fair to see;
And for the words the Queen had spoke
    Young Waters he did dee.

GLENLOGIE

1. FOUR-AND-TWENTY nobles rade to the King's ha',
But bonny Glenlogie was the flow'r o' them a'.

2. Lady Jeanie Melville cam' trippin' down the
    stair;
When she saw Glenlogie her hairt it grew sair.

3. She call'd to the footman that ran by his side:
   Says, 'What is your lord's name, an' where does
   he bide?'—

4. 'His name is Glenlogie when he is from home:
   He's of the gay Gordons, his name it is John.'—

5. 'Glenlogie, Glenlogie, an you will prove kind,
   My love is laid on you; I am tellin' my mind.'—

6. He turn'd about lightly, as the Gordons do a';
   Says, 'I thank you, Lady Jeanie, but I'm
   promised awa'.'

7. She call'd on her maidens her bed for to make,
   Her rings from her fingers she did them a' break.

8. 'Where will I get a bonny boy, to win hose and
   shoon,
   To go to Glenlogie and bid Logie come?'

9. When Glenlogie got the letter, amang noblemen,
   'I wonder,' said Glenlogie, 'what does young
   women mean?

10. 'I wonder i' the warld what women see at me,
    That bonny Jeanie Melville for my sake shou'd
    dee?

11. 'O what is my lineage, or what is my make,
    That bonny Jeanie Melville shou'd dee for my
    sake?

12. 'Go saddle my black horse, go saddle him soon,
    Till I ride to Bethelnie, to see Lady Jean!'

13. When he came to Bethelnie, he rade round about,
    And he saw Jeanie's father at the window look
        out.

14. When he came to the gateway, small mirth was
        there;
    But was weepin' and wailin', a' tearin' their hair.

15. O pale and wan look'd she when Glenlogie came
        ben,
    But red ruddy grew she whene'er he sat down.

16. 'Turn round, Jeanie Melville, turn round to this
        side,
    And I'll be the bridegroom, and you'll be the
        bride!'

17. O 'twas a merry weddin', and the portion down
        told,
    Of bonny Jeanie Melville, scarce sixteen years
        old!

LADY ELSPAT

1. 'O brent's your brow, my Lady Elspat;
       O gowden yellow is your hair!
    Of a' the maids o' fair Scotland
       There's nane like Lady Elspat fair.'

2. 'Perform your vows,' she says, 'Sweet William;
    The vows which ye ha' made to me;
And at the back o' my mither's castle
    This night I'll surely meet wi' thee.'

3. But wae be to her brother's page,
    Wha heard the words this twa did say!
He's tauld them to her lady mither,
    Wha wrought Sweet William mickle wae.

4. For she's ta'en him, Sweet William,
    And she's gar'd bind him wi's bow-string.
Till the red blood o' his fair body
    Frae ilka nail o' his hand did spring.

5. O it fell ance upon a time
    That the Lord Justice came to town;
Out she has ta'en him, Sweet William,
    Brought him before the Lord Justice boun'.

6. 'And what is the crime now, madame,' he says,
    'Has been committed by this young man?'—
'O he has broken my bonny castle,
    That was well biggit wi' lime and stane.

7. 'And he has broken my bonny coffers,
    That was well bandit wi' aiken ban';
And he has stolen my rich jewels;
    I wot he has them every ane.'

8. Then out it spak' her Lady Elspat
    As she sat by the Lord Justice' knee:
'Now ye hae tauld your tale, mither,
    I pray, Lord Justice, you'll now hear me.

9. 'He hasna broken her bonny castle,
    That was well biggit wi' lime and stane;
Nor has he stolen her rich jewels,
    For I wot she has them every one.

10. 'But tho' he was my first true love,
    And tho' I had sworn to be his bride,
'Cause he had not a great estate
    She would this way our loves divide.'

11. Then out it spak' the Lord Justice
    (I wot the tear was in his e'e):
'I see nae fault in this young man;
    Sae loose his bands, and set him free.

12. 'Tak' back your love now, Lady Elspat,
    And my best blessing you baith upon!
For gin he be your first true love,
    He is my eldest sister's son.

13. 'There is a steed within my stable
    Cost me baith gowd and white monèy;
Ye'se get as mickle o' my free land
    As he'll ride about in a summer's day.'

KATHARINE JOHNSTONE

1. THERE was a may, and a weel-far'd may,
   Lived high up in yon glen;
   Her name was Katharine Johnstone:
   She was courted by mony men.

2. Doun cam' the Laird o' Lamington
   Out frae the North Countrie,
   All for to court this pretty may,
   Her bridegroom for to be.

3. He tell'd na her father, he tell'd na her mither,
   He tell'd na ane o' her kin,
   But he tell'd the bonnie lass hersel'
   An' her consent did win.

4. But up then cam' Lord Faughanwood
   Out frae the English Border,
   And for to court this pretty may,
   A' mounted in good order.

5. He's tell'd her father, he's tell'd her mither,
   And a' the lave o' her kin;
   But he's tell'd na the bonny lass hersel'
   Till on her weddin'-e'en.

6. She's sent unto her first fere love,
   Gin he would come to see,
   And Lamington has sent back word
   Weel answer'd should she be.

7. Then he has sent a messenger
   Right quietly thro' the land,
   For four-and-twenty armèd men
   To ride at his command.

8. The bridegroom from a high window
   Beheld baith dale and down,
   And there he spied her first fere love
   Cam' riding to the toun.

9. She scoffèd and she scornèd him
   Upon her weddin'-day,
   And said it was the Fairy Court
   He saw in sic array!

10. When a' were at the dinner set,
    Drinking the blude-red wine,
    In cam' the Laird o' Lamington
    The bridegroom 'should hae been.

11. 'O come ye here to fight, young lord?
    Or come ye here to play?
    Or come ye here to drink good wine
    Upon the weddin'-day?'—

12. 'I come na here to fight,' he said,
    'I come na here to play;
    I'll but lead a dance wi' the bonny bride,
    And mount and go my way.'

13. There was a glass of the blude-red wine
  Was fill'd them up between,
 But aye she drank to Lamington,
  Wha her true love had been.

14. He's ta'en her by the milk-white hand,
  And by the grass-green sleeve;
 He's mounted her high behind himsel',
  At her kin he's spier'd nae leave.

15. There were four-and-twenty bonny boys
  A' clad in the Johnstone grey,
 They swore they would tak' the bride again
  By the strong hand, if they may.

16. It's up, it's up the Cowden bank,
  It's down the Cowden brae;
 The bride she gar'd the trumpet sound
  'It is a weel-won play!'

17. The blude ran down by Cowden bank
  And down by Cowden brae,
 But aye she gar'd the trumpet sound
  'It's a' fair play!'

18. 'My blessing on your heart, sweet thing!
  Wae to your wilfu' will!
 Sae mony a gallant gentleman's blood
  This day as ye've gar'd spill.'

19. But a' you lords of fair England,
     If you be English born,
   Come never to Scotland to seek a wife
     Or else ye'll get the scorn.

20. They'll haik ye up, and settle ye by,
     Until your weddin'-day;
   Then gie ye frogs instead o' fish,
     And do ye foul, foul play.

JOHNIE ARMSTRONG

1. Sum speiks of lords, sum speiks of lairds,
     And sick lyke men of hie degrie;
   Of a gentleman I sing a sang,
     Sum tyme called Laird of Gilnockie.

2. The King he wrytes a luving letter,
     With his ain hand sae tenderly,
   And he hath sent it to Johnie Armstrang,
     To cum and speik with him speedily.

3. The Eliots and Armstrangs did convene;
     They were a gallant cumpanie —
   'We'll ride and meit our lawful King,
     And bring him safe to Gilnockie.'

4. 'Make kinnen and capon ready, then,
     And venison in great plentie;

We'll wellcum here our royal King;
 I hope he'll dine at Gilnockie!'—

5. They ran their horse on the Langholme howm,
  And brak their spears wi' mickle main;
 The ladies lukit frae their loft windows —
  'God bring our men weel hame agen!'

6. When Johnie cam' before the King,
  Wi' a' his men sae brave to see,
 The King he movit his bonnet to him;
  He ween'd he was King as weel as he.

7. 'May I find grace, my sovereign liege,
  Grace for my loyal men and me?
 For my name it is Johnie Armstrang,
  And a subject of yours, my liege,' said he.

8. 'Away, away, thou traitor strang!
  Out o' my sight soon mayst thou be!
 I grantit never a traitor's life,
  And now I'll not begin wi' thee.'—

9. 'Grant me my life, my liege, my King!
  And a bonny gift I'll gie to thee:
 Full four-and-twenty milk-white steids,
  Were a' foal'd in ae yeir to me.

10. 'I'll gie thee a' these milk-white steids,
  That prance and nicker at a speir;

And as mickle gude Inglish gilt,
　As four o' their braid backs dow bear.'—

11. 'Away, away, thou traitor strang!
　　Out o' my sight soon mayst thou be!
　I grantit never a traitor's life,
　　And now I'll not begin wi' thee!'—

12. 'Grant me my life, my liege, my King!
　　And a bonny gift I'll gie to thee:
　Gude four-and-twenty ganging mills,
　　That gang thro' a' the yeir to me.

13. 'These four-and-twenty mills complete
　　Sall gang for thee thro' a' the yeir;
　And as mickle of gude reid wheit,
　　As a' thair happers dow to bear.'—

14. 'Away, away, thou traitor strang!
　　Out o' my sight soon mayst thou be!
　I grantit never a traitor's life,
　　And now I'll not begin wi' thee.'—

15. 'Grant me my life, my liege, my King!
　　And a great great gift I'll gie to thee:
　Bauld four-and-twenty sisters' sons,
　　Sall for thee fetch, tho' a' should flee!'—

16. 'Away, away, thou traitor strang!
　　Out o' my sight soon mayst thou be!

I grantit never a traitor's life,
And now I'll not begin wi' thee.'—

17. 'Grant me my life, my liege, my King!
And a brave gift I'll gie to thee:
All between heir and Newcastle town
Sall pay their yeirly rent to thee.'—

18. 'Away, away, thou traitor strang!
Out o' my sight soon mayst thou be!
I grantit never a traitor's life,
And now I'll not begin wi' thee.'—

19. 'Ye lied, ye lied, now, King,' he says,
'Altho' a King and Prince ye be!
For I've luved naething in my life,
I weel dare say it, but honesty:

20. 'Save a fat horse, and a fair woman,
Twa bonny dogs to kill a deir;
But England suld have found me meal and
mault,
Gif I had lived this hundred yeir!

21. 'She suld have found me meal and mault,
And beef and mutton in a' plentie;
But never a Scots wyfe could have said
That e'er I skaith'd her a puir flee.

22. 'To seik het water beneith cauld ice,
Surely it is a greit folie —

    I have asked grace at a graceless face,
        But there is nane for my men and me!

23. 'But had I kenn'd ere I cam' frae hame,
        How thou unkind wadst been to me!
    I wad have keepit the Border side,
        In spite of all thy force and thee.

24. 'Wist England's King that I was ta'en,
        O gin a blythe man he wad be!
    For anes I slew his sister's son,
        And on his breist bane brak a trie.'

25. John wore a girdle about his middle,
        Imbroider'd owre wi' burning gold,
    Bespangled wi' the same metal,
        Maist beautiful was to behold.

26. There hung nine targats at Johnie's hat,
        And ilk ane worth three hundred pound —
  'What wants that knave that a King suld have,
        But the sword of honour and the crown?

27. 'O where got thou these targats, Johnie,
        That blink sae brawlie abune thy brie?'—
  'I gat them in the field fechting,
        Where, cruel King, thou durst not be.

28. 'Had I my horse, and harness gude.
    And riding as I wont to be,

It suld have been told this hundred yeir,
    The meeting of my King and me!

29. 'God be with thee, Kirsty, my brother,
    Lang live thou Laird of Mangertoun!
Lang mayst thou live on the Border syde,
    Ere thou see thy brother ride up and doun!

30. 'And God be with thee, Kirsty, my son,
    Where thou sits on thy nurse's knee!
But an thou live this hundred yeir,
    Thy father's better thou'lt never be.

31. 'Farewell! my bonny Gilnock hall,
    Where on Esk side thou standest stout!
Gif I had lived but seven yeirs mair,
    I wad hae gilt thee round about.'

32. John murder'd was at Carlinrigg,
    And all his gallant companie;
But Scotland's heart was ne'er sae wae,
    To see sae mony brave men die —

33. Because they saved their country deir
    Frae Englishmen! Nane were sa bauld,
Whyle Johnie lived on the Border syde,
    Nane of them durst cum neir his hauld.

CLYDE WATER

1. WILLIE stands in his stable door,
   And clapping at his steed,
   And over his white fingers
   His nose began to bleed.

2. 'Gie corn unto my horse, mither,
   Gie meat unto my man;
   For I maun gang to Margaret's bour
   Before the nicht comes on.'—

3. 'O bide at hame this nicht, Willie,
   This ae bare nicht wi' me:
   The bestan bed in a' my house
   Sall be well made to thee.

4. 'O bide at hame this nicht, Willie,
   This ae bare nicht wi' me:
   The bestan bird in a' the roost
   At your supper, son, sall be.'—

5. 'A' your beds and a' your roosts
   I value not a pin;
   But I sall gae to my love's gates
   This nicht, gif I can win.'—

6. 'O stay at home, my son Willie,
   The wind blaws cauld an' sour;
   The nicht will be baith mirk and late
   Before ye reach her bour.'—

7. 'O though the nicht were ever sae dark,
   Or the wind blew never sae cauld,
  I will be in my Margaret's bour
   Before twa hours be tald.'—

8. 'O an ye gang to Margaret's bour
   Sae sair against my will,
  I' the deepest pot o' Clyde's water
   My malison ye'se feel.'

9. As he rade owre yon high high hill,
   And doun yon dowie den,
  The roaring that was in Clyde's water
   Wad fley'd five hundred men.

10. His heart was warm, his pride was up,
   Sweet Willie kentna fear;
  But yet his mither's malison
   Aye soundit in his ear.

11. 'O spare, O spare me, Clyde's water!
   Your stream rins wondrous strang:
  Mak' me your wrack as I come back,
   But spare me as I gang!'

12. Then he rade in, and further in,
   And he swam to an' fro,
  Until he's grippit a hazel bush
   That brung him to the brow.

13. Then he is on to Margaret's bour,
    And tirlèd at the pin;
    But doors were steek'd and windows barr'd,
    And nane wad let him in.

14. 'O open the door to me, Marg'ret!
    O open and let me in!
    For my boots are fu' o' Clyde's water
    And the rain rins owre my chin.'—

15. 'I darena open the door to you,
    Nor darena let you in;
    For my mither she is fast asleep,
    And I maun mak' nae din.'—

16. 'O hae ye ne'er a stable?' he says,
    'Or hae ye ne'er a barn?
    Or hae ye ne'er a wild-goose house
    Where I might rest till morn?'—

17. 'My barn it is fu' o' corn,' she says,
    'My stable is fu' o' hay;
    My house is fu' o' merry young men;
    They winna remove till day.'—

18. 'O fare ye weel then, May Marg'ret,
    Sin' better may na be!
    I've gotten my mither's malison
    This nicht, coming to thee.'

19. He's mounted on his coal-black steed,
 — O but his heart was wae!
But ere he came to Clyde's water
 'Twas half up owre the brae.

20. 'An hey, Willie! an hoa, Willie!
 Winna ye turn agen?'
Buy aye the louder that she cried
 He rade agenst the win'.

21. As he rade owre yon high high hill,
 And doun yon dowie den,
The roaring that was in Clyde's water
 Wad fley'd a thousand men.

22. He rade in, and farther in,
 Till he cam' to the chine;
The rushing that was in Clyde's water
 Took Willie's riding-cane.

23. He lean'd him owre his saddle-bow
 To catch the rod by force;
The rushing that was in Clyde's water
 Took Willie frae his horse.

24. 'O how can I turn my horse's head?
 How can I learn to sowm?
I've gotten my mither's malison,
 And it's here that I maun drown!'

25. O he swam high, and he swam low,
    And he swam to and fro,
    But he couldna spy the hazel-bush
    Wad bring him to the brow.

26. He's sunk and he never rase agen
    Into the pot sae deep . . .
    And up it waken'd May Margaret
    Out o' her drowsie sleep.

27. 'Come hither, come here, my mither dear,
    Read me this dreary dream;
    I dream'd my Willie was at our gates,
    And nane wad let him in.'—

28. 'Lie still, lie still now, my Meggie:∙
    Lie still and tak' your rest;
    Sin' your true-love was at your gates
    It's but twa quarters past.'—

29. Nimbly, nimbly rase she up,
    And nimbly put she on;
    And the higher that the lady cried,
    The louder blew the win'.

30. The firstan step that she stept in,
    She steppit to the queet:
    'Ohon, alas!' said that lady,
    'This water's wondrous deep.'

31. The neistan step that she stept in,
　　　She waded to the knee;
　　Says she, 'I cou'd wade farther in,
　　　If I my love cou'd see.'

32. The neistan step that she wade in,
　　　She waded to the chin;
　　The deepest pot in Clyde's water
　　　She got sweet Willie in.

33. 'Ye've had a cruel mither, Willie!
　　　And I have had anither;
　　But we sall sleep in Clyde's water
　　　Like sister an' like brither.'

ANNAN WATER

1. ANNAN water's wading deep,
　　　And my love Annie's wondrous bonny;
　　And I am laith she suld weet her feet,
　　　Because I love her best of ony.

2. 'Gar saddle me the bonny black,
　　　Gar saddle sune, and make him ready;
　　For I will down the Gatehope-Slack,
　　　And all to see my bonny ladye.'

3. He has loupen on the bonny black,
　　　He stirr'd him wi' the spur right sairly;

But, or he wan the Gatehope-Slack,
    I think the steed was wae and weary.

4. He has loupen on the bonny grey,
    He rade the right gate and the ready;
I trow he would neither stint nor stay,
    For he was seeking his bonny ladye.

5. O he has ridden o'er field and fell,
    Through muir and moss, and mony a mire:
His spurs o' steel were sair to bide,
    And frae her fore-feet flew the fire.

6. 'Now, bonny grey, now play your part!
    Gin ye be the steed that wins my deary,
Wi' corn and hay ye'se be fed for aye,
    And never spur sall make you wearie.'

7. The grey was a mare, and a right good mare;
    But when she wan the Annan water,
She couldna hae ridden a furlong mair,
    Had a thousand merks been wadded at her.

8. 'O boatman, boatman, put off your boat!
    Put off your boat for gowden money!
I cross the drumly stream the night,
    Or never mair I see my honey.'—

9. 'O I was sworn sae late yestreen,
    And not by ae aith, but by many;

And for a' the gowd in fair Scotland,
 I dare na take ye through to Annie.'—

10. The side was stey, and the bottom deep,
 Frae bank to brae the water pouring;
And the bonny grey mare did sweat for fear,
 For she heard the water-kelpy roaring.

11. O he has pu'd aff his dapperpy coat,
 The silver buttons glanced bonny;
The waistcoat bursted aff his breast,
 He was sae full of melancholy.

12. He has ta'en the ford at that stream tail;
 I wot he swam both strong and steady,
But the stream was broad, and his strength
  did fail,
 And he never saw his bonny ladye!

13. O wae betide the frush saugh wand!
 And wae betide the bush of brier!
It brake into my true love's hand,
 When his strength did fail, and his limbs
  did tire.

14. 'And wae betide ye, Annan Water,
 This night that ye are a drumlie river!
For over thee I'll build a bridge,
 That ye never more true love may sever.'—

RARE WILLY DROWNED IN YARROW

1. 'WILLY's rare, and Willy's fair,
    And Willy's wondrous bonny;
And Willy heght to marry me,
    Gin e'er he marryd ony.

2. 'Yestreen I made my bed fu' braid,
    The night I'll make it narrow,
For a' the live-long winter's night
    I lie twin'd of my marrow.

3. 'O came you by yon water-side?
    Pu'd you the rose or lilly?
Or came you by yon meadow green?
    Or saw you my sweet Willy?'

4. She sought him east, she sought him west,
    She sought him braid and narrow;
Sine, in the clifting of a craig,
    She found him drown'd in Yarrow.

THE DUKE OF GORDON'S DAUGHTER

1. The Duke of Gordon had three daughters,
    Elizabeth, Marg'ret and Jean;
They would not stay in bonny Castle
       Gordon,
    But they went to bonny Aberdeen.

2. They had not been in bonny Aberdeen
   A twelvemonth and a day,
   Lady Jean fell in love with Captain Ogilvie
   And awa' with him she would gae.

3. Word came to the Duke of Gordon,
   In the chamber where he lay,
   Lady Jean was in love with Captain Ogilvie,
   And from him she would not stay.

4. 'Go saddle to me the black horse,
   And you'll ride on the grey,
   And I will gang to bonny Aberdeen
   Forthwith to bring her away.'

5. They were not a mile from Aberdeen,
   A mile but only one,
   Till he met with his two daughters,
   But awa' was Lady Jean.

6. 'Where is your sister, maidens?
   Where is your sister now?
   Say, what is become of your sister,
   That she is not walking with you?'

7. 'O pardon us, honor'd father,
   O pardon us!' they did say;
   'Lady Jean is wed with Captain Ogilvie,
   And from him she will not stay.'

8. Then an angry man the Duke rade on
     Till he came to bonny Aberdeen,
   And there did he see brave Captain Ogilvie
     A-training of his men on the green.

9. 'O woe be to thee, thou Captain Ogilvie!
     And an ill death thou shalt dee.
   For taking to thee my daughter Jean
     High hangit shalt thou be.'

10. The Duke has written a broad letter,
      To the King with his own han';
    It was to hang Captain Ogilvie
      If ever he hang'd a man.

11. 'I will not hang Captain Ogilvie
      For no lord that I see;
    But I'll gar him put off the broad scarlèt,
      And put on the single liverỳ.'

12. Now word came to Captain Ogilvie,
      In the chamber where he lay,
    To cast off the gold lace and scarlet,
      And put on the single liverỳ.

13. 'If this be for bonny Jeanie Gordon,
      This penance I can take wi';
    If this be for dear Jeanie Gordon,
      All this and mair will I dree.'

14. Lady Jeanie had not been married
    A year but only three,
Till she had a babe upon every arm
    And another upon her knee.

15. 'O but I'm weary of wand'rin'!
    O but my fortune is bad!
It sets not the Duke of Gordon's daughter
    To follow a soldier lad.

16. 'O but I'm weary, weary wand'rin'!
    O but I think it lang!
It sets not the Duke of Gordon's daughter
    To follow a single man.

17. 'O hold thy tongue, Jeanie Gordon,
    O hold thy tongue, my lamb!
For once I was a noble captain,
    Now for thy sake a single man.'

18. But when they came to the Highland hills,
    Cold was the frost and snow;
Lady Jean's shoes they were all torn,
    No farther could she go.

19. 'Now woe to the hills and the mountains!
    Woe to the wind and the rain!
My feet is sair wi' going barefoot:
    No farther can I gang.

20. 'O were I in the glens o' Foudlen,
    Where hunting I have been,
  I would go to bonny Castle Gordon,
    There I'd get hose and sheen!'

21. When they came to bonny Castle Gordon,
    And standing on the green,
  The porter out with loud loud shout,
    'O here comes our Lady Jean!'—

22. 'You are welcome, bonny Jeanie Gordon,
    You are dear welcome to me;
  You are welcome, dear Jeanie Gordon,
    But awa' with your Ogilvie!'

23. Over-seas now went the Captain,
    As a soldier under command;
  But a message soon follow'd after,
    To come home for to heir his land.

24. 'O what does this mean?' says the Captain;
    'Where's my brother's children three?'—
  'They are a' o' them dead and buried:
    Come home, pretty Captain Ogilvie!'

25. 'Then hoist up your sail,' says the Captain,
    'And we'll hie back owre the sea;
  And I'll gae to bonny Castle Gordon,
    There my dear Jeanie to see.'

26. He came to bonny Castle Gordon,
        And upon the green stood he:
    The porter out with a loud loud shout,
        'Here comes our Captain Ogilvie!'—

27. 'You're welcome, pretty Captain Ogilvie,
        Your fortune's advanced, I hear;
    No stranger can come to my castle
        That I do love so dear.'—

28. 'Put up your hat, Duke of Gordon;
        Let it fa' not from your head.
    It never set the noble Duke of Gordon
        To bow to a single soldier lad.

29. 'Sir, the last time I was at your Castle,
        You would not let me in;
    Now I'm come for my wife and children,
        No friendship else I claim.'

30. Down the stair Lady Jean came tripping,
        With the saut tear in her e'e;
    She had a babe in every arm,
        And another at her knee.

31. The Captain took her straight in his arms,
        — O a happy man was he! —
    Saying, 'Welcome, bonny Jeanie Gordon,
        My Countess o' Cumberland to be!'

THE BONNY EARL OF MURRAY

1. YE Highlands and ye Lawlands,
     O where hae ye been?
   They hae slain the Earl of Murray,
     And hae laid him on the green.

2. Now wae be to thee, Huntley!
     And whairfore did ye sae!
   I bade you bring him wi' you,
     But forbade you him to slay.

3. He was a braw gallant,
     And he rid at the ring;
   And the bonny Earl of Murray,
     O he might hae been a king!

4. He was a braw gallant,
     And he play'd at the ba';
   And the bonny Earl of Murray
     Was the flower amang them a'!

5. He was a braw gallant,
     And he play'd at the gluve;
   And the bonny Earl of Murray,
     O he was the Queen's luve!

6. O lang will his Lady
     Look owre the Castle Downe,
   Ere she see the Earl of Murray
     Come sounding through the town!

BONNY GEORGE CAMPBELL

1. HIE upon Hielands,
      And laigh upon Tay,
   Bonny George Campbell
      Rade out on a day:
   Saddled and bridled,
      Sae gallant to see,
   Hame cam' his gude horse,
      But never cam' he.

2. Down ran his auld mither,
      Greetin' fu' sair;
   Out ran his bonny bride,
      Reaving her hair;
   'My meadow lies green,
      And my corn is unshorn,
   My barn is to bigg,
      And my babe is unborn.'

3. Saddled and bridled
      And booted rade he;
   A plume in his helmet,
      A sword at his knee;
   But toom cam' his saddle
      A' bluidy to see,
   O hame cam' his gude horse,
      But never cam' he!

BOOK IV

ROBIN HOOD AND GUY OF GISBORNE

1. WHEN shaws beene sheene, and shradds full
        fayre,
    And leves both large and longe,
  Itt is merrye walking in the fayre forrèst
    To heare the small birds' songe.

2. The woodweele sang, and wold not cease,
    Sitting upon the spraye,
  Soe lowde, he wakened Robin Hood,
    In the grenewood where he lay.

3. 'Now by my faye,' sayd jollye Robin.
    'A sweaven I had this night;
  I dreamt me of two wight yemen,
    That fast with me can fight.

4. 'Methought they did mee beate and binde
    And tooke my bow mee fro;
  If I be Robin alive in this lande,
    I'll be wroken on them towe.'

5. 'Sweavens are swift, Master,' quoth John,
    'As the wind that blowes ore a hill;

For if itt be never so loude this night,
   To-morrow itt may be still.'

6. 'Buske yee, bowne yee, my merry men all,
      And John shall goe with mee,
   For I'le goe seeke yond wight yemen,
      In grenewood where they bee.'

7. They cast on them their gownes of grene,
      And tooke theyr bowes each one;
   And all away to the grene forrèst
      A shooting forth are gone;

8. Until they came to the merry grenewood,
      Where they had gladdest bee,
   There were they ware of a wight yemàn,
      His body lean'd to a tree.

9. A sword and a dagger he wore by his side,
      Of manye a man the bane;
   And he was clad in his capull-hyde,
      Topp and tayll and mayne.

10. 'Stand you still, Master,' quoth Little John,
      'Under this trusty tree,
   And I will go to yond wight yeoman
      To know his meaning trulye.'

11. 'A! John, by me thou settest noe store,
      And that's a farley finde.

How offt send I my men beffore,
And tarry my selfe behinde?

12. 'It is noe cunning a knave to ken,
An a man but heare him speake;
An itt were not for bursting of my bowe,
John, I wold thy head breake.'

13. As often wordes they breeden bale,
So they parted Robin and John:
And John is gone to Barnèsdale;
The gates he knoweth eche one.

14. But when he came to Barnèsdale,
Great heavinesse there hee hadd,
For he found two of his owne fellòwes
Were slaine both in a slade.

15. And Scarlette à-foote he flyinge was
Fast over stocke and stone,
For the Sheriffe with seven score men
Fast after him is gone.

16. 'Yet one shoote I'le shoote,'quoth Little John,
'With Christ his might and mayne;
I'le make yond fellow that flyes soe fast,
To stopp he shall be fayne.'

17. Then John bent up his good yewe-bowe
And fettl'd him to shoote:

The bow was made of a tender boughe,
    And fell downe to his foote.

18. 'Woe worth thee, wicked wood,' sayd John,
    'That ere thou grew on a tree!
For now this day thou art my bale,
    My boote when thou shold bee.'

19. His shoote it was but loosely shott,
    Yet it flewe not in vaine,
For itt met one of the Sherriff's men,
    Good William à Trent was slaine.

20. It had bene better of William à Trent
    To have hangèd upon a gallòw,
Than to be that day in the grene-wood
    To meet Little John's arrowe.

21. But as it is said, when men be mett
    Fyve can doe more than three,
The Sheriffe hath taken Little John,
    And bound him fast to a tree.

22. 'Thou shalt be drawen by dale and downe,
    And hangèd hye on a hill.'—
'But thou mayst fayle,' quoth Little John,
    'If itt be Christ his will.'

23. Let us leave talking of Little John,
    And thinke of Robin Hood,

How he is gone to the wight yemàn,
   Where under the leaves he stood.

24. 'Good morrowe, good fellowe,' sayd Robin so
         fayre,
      'Good morrowe, good fellow,' quoth he:
   'Methinks by this bowe thou beares in thy
         hande
      A good archere thou sholdst bee.'

25. 'I am wilful of my waye,' quo' the yeman,
      'And of my morning tyde.'
   'I'le lead thee through the wood,' sayd Robin;
      'Good fellow, I'le be thy guide.'

26. 'I seeke an outlàwe,' the straunger sayd,
      'Men call him Robin Hood;
   Rather I'ld meet with that proud outlàwe,
      Than fortye pound of go'd.'—

27. 'If you two met, it wold be seene
      Whether were better man:
   But let us under the levès grene
      Some other pastime plan.

28. 'Let us some other masteryes make
      Among the woods so even,
   Wee may chance meet with Robin Hood
      Here att some unsett steven.'

29. They cutt them downe two summer shroggs,
    That grew both under a breere,
And sett them threescore rood in twinne
    To shoot the prickes y-fere.

30. 'Leade on, good fellowe,' quoth Robin Hood,
    'Leade on, I doe bidd thee.'—
'Nay by my faith, good fellowe,' hee sayd,
    'My leader thou shalt bee.'

31. The first good shot that Robin led,
    He mist but an inch it fro':
The yeoman he was an archer good,
    But he cold ne'er shoote soe. ·

32. The second shoote had the wight yemàn,
    He shote within the garlànde:
But Robin he shott far better than hee,
    For he clave the good pricke wande.

33. 'God's blessing upon thy heart!' he sayd;
    'Good fellowe, thy shooting is goode;
For an thy hart be as good as thy hand,
    Thou wert better than Robin Hood.'

34. 'Now tell me thy name, good fellowe,' sayd he,
    'Under the leaves of lyne.'—
'Nay by my faith,' quoth good Robin,
    'Till thou have told me thine.'

35. 'I dwell by dale and downe,' quoth hee,
    'And Robin to take I'me sworne;
  And when I am callèd by my right name
    I am Guy of good Gisborne.'—

36. 'My dwelling is in this wood,' sayes Robin,
    'By thee I set right nought:
  I am Robin Hood of Barnèsdale,
    Whom thou so long hast sought.'

37. He that had neither beene kithe nor kin,
    Might have seene a full fayre sight,
  To see how together these yemen went
    With blades both browne and bright:

38. To see how these yemen together they fought
    Two howres of a summer's day:
  Yett neither Sir Guy nor Robin Hood
    Them fettled to flye away.

39. Robin was reachles on a roote,
    And stumbled at that tyde;
  And Guy was quick and nimble with-all,
    And hitt him o'er the left side.

40. 'Ah deere Lady!' sayd Robin Hood,
    'That art both mother and may,
  I think it was never man's destinye
    To dye before his day.'

41. Robin thought on Our Ladye deere,
  And soone leapt up againe,
 And strait he came with an aukward stroke,
  And he Sir Guy hath slayne.

42. He took Sir Guy's head by the hayre,
  And stickèd itt on his bowes end:
 'Thou hast been traytor all thy life,
  Which thing must have an ende.'

43. Robin pulled forth an Irish kniffe,
  And nicked Sir Guy in the face,
 That he was never on woman born,
  Cold tell whose head it was.

44. Saies, 'Lye there, lye there, good Sir Guy,
  And with me be not wrothe;
 If thou have had the worse strokes at my
   hand
  Thou shalt have the better clothe.'

45. Robin did off his gowne of greene,
  And on Sir Guy did it throwe,
 And he put on that capull-hyde,
  That clad him topp to toe.

46. 'The bowe, the arrowes, and litle horne,
  Now with me I will beare;
 For I will away to Barnèsdale,
  To see how my men doe fare.'

47. Robin sett Guy's horne to his mouth,
    A loud blast in it he did blow.
  That beheard the Sheriffe of Nottingham,
    As he leaned under a lowe.

48. 'Hearken! hearken!' sayd the Sheriffe,
    'I heare now tydings good,
  For yonder I heare Sir Guy's horne blowe,
    And he hath slaine Robin Hood.'

49. 'Yonder I heare Sir Guy's horne blowe,
    Itt blowes soe well in tyde,
  And yonder comes that wight yemàn,
    Cladd in his capull-hyde.

50. 'Come hyther, come hyther, thou good Sir
    Guy,
    Aske what thou wilt of mee.'—
  'O I will none of thy gold,' sayd Robin,
    'Nor I will none of thy fee:

51. 'But now I have slaine the master,' he sayes,
    'Let me go strike the knave;
  This is all the rewarde I aske;
    Nor noe other will I have.'

52. 'Thou art a madman,' said the Sheriffe,
    'Thou sholdest have had a knight's fee:
  But seeing thy asking hath beene so bad
    Well granted it shall be.'

53. When Little John heard his master speake,
    Well knewe he it was his steven:
  'Now shall I be looset,' quoth Little John,
    'With Christ his might in heaven.'

54. Robin hee hyed him to Little John,
    He thought to loose him belive;
  The Sheriffe and all his companye
    Fast after him did drive.

55. 'Stand abacke! stand abacke!' sayd Robin
    Hood;
    'Why draw you mee soe neere?
  Itt was never the use in our countrye,
    One's shrift another shold heere.'

56. But Robin pull'd forth an Irysh kniffe,
    And losed John hand and foote,
  And gave him Sir Guy's bow into his hand,
    And bade it be his boote.

57. Then John he took Guy's bow in his hand,
    His boltes and arrowes eche one:
  When the Sheriffe saw Little John bend his
    bow,
    He fettled him to be gone.

58. Towards his house in Nottingham towne
    He fled full fast away;
  And soe did all his companye:
    Not one behind wold stay.

59. But he cold neither goe soe fast,
    Nor away soe fast cold runne,
  But Little John with an arrowe soe broad,
    Did cleave his herte in twinne.

ROBIN HOOD AND THE WIDOW'S THREE SONS

1. THERE are twelve months in all the year,
    As I hear many men say,
  But the merriest month in all the year
    Is the merry month of May.

2. Now Robin Hood is to Nottingham gone,
    With a link a down and a day,
  And there he met a silly old woman,
    Was weeping on the way.

3. 'What news? what news, thou silly old woman?
    What news hast thou for me?'
  Said she, 'There's three squires in Nottingham
      town
    To-day is condemn'd to die.'

4. 'O have they parishes burnt?' he said,
    'Or have they ministers slain?
  Or have they robb'd any virgin,
    Or other men's wives have ta'en?'—

5. 'They have no parishes burnt, good sir,
   Nor yet have ministers slain,
   Nor have they robbed any virgin,
   Nor other men's wives have ta'en.'

6. 'O what have they done?' said bold Robin Hood,
   'I pray thee tell to me.'—
   'It's for slaying of the King's fallow deer,
   Bearing their long bows with thee.'—

7. 'Dost thou not mind, old woman,' he said,
   'Since thou made me sup and dine?
   By the truth of my body,' quoth bold Robin
           Hood,
   'You could tell it in no better time.'

8. Now Robin Hood is to Nottingham gone,
   With a link a down and a day,
   And there he met with a silly old palmer,
   Was walking along the highway.

9. 'What news? what news, thou silly old man?
   What news, I do thee pray?'—
   Said he, 'Three squires in Nottingham town
   Are condemned to die this day.'—

10. 'Come change thy apparel with me, old man,
    Come change thy apparel for mine;
    Here is forty shillings in good silver,
    Go drink it in beer or wine.'—

11. 'O thine apparel is good,' he said,
    'And mine is ragged and torn;
  Wherever you go, wherever you ride,
    Laugh ne'er an old man to scorn.'—

12. 'Come change thy apparel with me, old churl,
    Come change thy apparel with mine;
  Here are twenty pieces of good broad gold,
    Go feast thy brethren with wine.'

13. Then he put on the old man's hat,
    It stood full high on the crown:
  'The first bold bargain that I come at,
    It shall make thee come down.'

14. Then he put on the old man's cloak,
    Was patch'd black, blue, and red;
  He thought no shame, all the day long,
    To wear the bags of bread.

15. Then he put on the old man's breeks,
    Was patch'd from ballup to side;
  'By the truth of my body,' bold Robin can say,
    'This man lov'd little pride!'

16. Then he put on the old man's hose,
    Were patch'd from knee to wrist;
  'By the truth of my body,' said bold Robin
      Hood,
    'I'd laugh if I had any list.'

17. Then he put on the old man's shoes,
     Were patch'd both beneath and aboon;
   Then Robin Hood swore a solemn oath,
     'It's good habit that makes a man!'

18. Now Robin Hood is to Nottingham gone,
     With a link a down and a down,
   And there he met with the proud Sheriff,
     Was walking along the town.

19. 'O save, O save, O Sheriff,' he said,
     'O save, and you may see!
   And what will you give to a silly old man
     To-day will your hangman be?'

20. 'Some suits, some suits,' the Sheriff he said,
     'Some suits I'll give to thee;
   Some suits, some suits, and pence thirteen
     To-day's a hangman's fee.'

21. Then Robin he turns him round about,
     And jumps from stock to stone;
   'By the truth of my body,' the Sheriff he said,
     'That's well jumpt, thou nimble old man.'—

22. 'I was ne'er a hangman in all my life,
     Nor yet intends to trade;
   But curst be he,' said bold Robin,
     'That first a hangman was made!

23. 'I've a bag for meal, and a bag for malt,
    And a bag for barley and corn;
 A bag for bread, and a bag for beef,
    And a bag for my little small horn.

24. 'I have a horn in my pockèt,
    I got it from Robin Hood,
 And still when I set it to my mouth,
    For thee it blows little good.'—

25. 'O wind thy horn, thou proud fellòw,
    Of thee I have no doubt;
 I wish that thou give such a blast
    Till both thy eyes fall out.'

26. The first loud blast that he did blow,
    He blew both loud and shrill;
 A hundred and fifty of Robin Hood's men
    Came riding over the hill.

27. The next loud blast that he did give,
    He blew both loud and amain;
 And quickly sixty of Robin Hood's men
    Came shining over the plain.

28. 'O who are yon,' the Sheriff he said,
    'Come tripping over the lee?'
 'They're my attendants,' brave Robin did say,
    'They'll pay a visit to thee.'

29. They took the gallows from the slack,
  They set it in the glen,
 They hang'd the proud Sheriff on that,
  And releas'd their own three men.

THE DEATH OF ROBIN HOOD

1. WHEN Robin Hood and Little John
  Down a-down, a-down, a-down,
 Went o'er yon bank of broom,
  Said Robin Hood bold to Little John,
 'We have shot for many a pound,
  Hey, down a-down, a-down!

2. 'But I am not able to shoot one shot more,
  My broad arrows will not flee;
 But I have a cousin lives down below,
  Please God, she will bleed me.

3. 'I will never eat nor drink,' he said,
  'Nor meat will do me good,
 Till I have been to merry Kirkleys
  My veins for to let blood.

4. 'The dame prior is my aunt's daughter,
  And nigh unto my kin;
 I know she wo'ld me no harm this day,
  For all the world to win.'

5. 'That I rede not,' said Little John,
    'Master, by th'assent of me,
Without half a hundred of your best
      bowmen
    You take to go with yee.'—

6. 'An thou be afear'd, thou Little John,
    At home I rede thee be.'—
'An you be wroth, my deare mastèr
    You shall never hear more of me.'

7. Now Robin is gone to merry Kirkleys
    And knockèd upon the pin:
Up then rose Dame Priorèss
    And let good Robin in.

8. Then Robin gave to Dame Priorèss
    Twenty pound in gold,
And bade her spend while that did last,
    She sho'ld have more when she wo'ld.

9. 'Will you please to sit down, cousin Robin,
    And drink some beer with me?'—
'No, I will neither eat nor drink
    Till I am blooded by thee.'

10. Down then came Dame Priorèss
    Down she came in that ilk,
With a pair of blood-irons in her hands
    Were wrappèd all in silk.

11. 'Set a chafing-dish to the fire,' she said,
    'And strip thou up thy sleeve.'
    — I hold him but an unwise man
      That will no warning 'leeve!

12. She laid the blood-irons to Robin's vein,
    Alack, the more pitye!
    And pierc'd the vein, and let out the blood
      That full red was to see.

13. And first it bled the thick, thick blood,
    And afterwards the thin,
    And well then wist good Robin Hood
      Treason there was within.

14. And there she blooded bold Robin Hood
    While one drop of blood wou'd run;
    Where did he bleed the live-long day,
      Until the next at noon.

15. He bethought him then of a casement there,
    Being lockèd up in the room;
    But was so weak he could not leap,
      He could not get him down.

16. He bethought him then of his bugle-horn,
    That hung low down to his knee;
    He set his horn unto his mouth,
      And blew out weak blasts three.

17. Then Little John he heard the horn
    Where he sat under a tree:
    'I fear my master is now near dead,
    He blows so wearilye.'

18. Little John is gone to merry Kirkleys,
    As fast as he can dree;
    And when he came to merry Kirkleys,
    He broke locks two or three:

19. Until he came bold Robin to see,
    Then he fell on his knee;
    'A boon, a boon!' cries Little John,
    'Master, I beg of thee!'

20. 'What is that boon,' said Robin Hood,
    'Little John, thou begs of me?'—
    'It is to burn fair Kirkleys-hall,
    And all their nunnerye.'

21. 'Now nay, now nay,' quoth Robin Hood,
    'That boon I'll not grant thee;
    I never hurt woman in all my life,
    Nor men in their company.

22. 'I never hurt maid in all my time,
    Nor at mine end shall it be;
    But give me my bent bow in my hand,
    And a broad arrow I'll let flee;
    And where this arrow is taken up
    There shall my grave digg'd be.

23. 'But lay me a green sod under my head,
    And another at my feet;
And lay my bent bow at my side,
    Which was my music sweet;
And make my grave of gravel and green,
    Which is most right and meet.

24. 'Let me have length and breadth enough,
    And under my head a sod;
That they may say when I am dead,
    — *Here lies bold Robin Hood!*'

BOOK V

DURHAM FIELD

1. LORDINGS, listen, and hold you still;
   Hearken to me a spell;
   I shall you tell of the fairest battell
   That ever in England befell.

2. It befell in Edward the Third's dayes,
   When in England he ware the crowne,
   That all the chief chivalry of England
   They buskèd and made them bowne.

3. They have chosen all the best archers
   That in England might be found,
   And all was to fight with the King of France,
   Within a litle stounde.

4. And when our King was over the water,
   And on the salt sea gone,
   Then tydings into Scotland came
   That all England was gone.

5. Bowes and arrowes they all were forth;
   At home was not left a man
   But shepards and millers both,
   And preists with shaven crownes.

6. Then the King of Scotts in a study stood,
      As he was a man of great might;
   He sware he would hold his parlament in leeve
         London,
      If he cold ryde there right.

7. Then bespake a Squire, of Scottland borne,
      And sayd, 'My leege, ha' peace,
   Before you come to leeve London,
      Full sore you'le rue that race.

8. 'Ther beene bold yeomen in merry England,
      Husbandmen stiffe and strong;
   Sharpè swords they done weare,
      Bearen bowes and arrowes longe.'

9. The King was angrye at that word;
      A long sword out he drew,
   And there before his royall companye
      His ownè Squire hee slew.

10. Hard hansell had the Scottes that day,
      That wrought them woe enoughe,
   Ffor a Scott then durst not speake a word
      For hanging att a boughe.

11. 'The Earle of Anguish, where art thou?
      In my coate-armour thou shalt bee,
   And thou shalt lead the forward
      Thorow the English countrye.

12. 'Take thee Yorke,' then sayd the King,
    'In stead wheras it doth stand;
  I'le make thy eldest sonne after thee
    Heyre of all Northumberland.

13. 'The Earle of Buchan, where be yee?
    In my coate-armour thou shalt bee;
  The high Peak and all Darbyshire
    I give it thee to thy fee.'

14. The famous Douglas then came in,
    Saies, 'What shall my meede bee?
  And I will lead the vanward, lord,
    Thorow the English countrye.'

15. 'Take thee Worster,' sayd the King,
    'Tuxburye, Killingworth, Burton on Trent;
  Doe thou not say another day
    But I gave thee lands and rent.

16. 'Sir Richard of Edenborrow, where are yee?
    A wise man in this warr!
  I'le give thee Bristow and the shire
    The time that wee come there.

17. 'Thou, my lord Nevill, where art thou?
    Thou must in this warres bee;
  I'le give thee Shrewsburye,' saies the King,
    'And Coventrye faire and free.

18. 'My lord of Hambleton, where art thou?
      Thou art of my kin full nye;
    I'le give thee Lincolne and Lincolneshire,
      And that's enoughe for thee.'

19. By then came in William Douglas,
      As breeme as any bore;
    He kneelèd him downe upon his knees,
      In his heart he sighèd sore.

20. 'I have servèd you, my lovelye liege,
      This thirty winters and four,
    And in the Scottish Marches
      Have beene wounded and beaten sore.

21. 'For all the good service that I have done,
      What now shall my meed bee?
    And I will lead the vanward
      Thorow the English countrye.'

22. 'Now aske on, Douglas,' said the King,
      'And granted it shall bee.'—
    'Why then, I aske litle London,' saies Douglas,
      'Gotten gif that it bee.'

23. The King was wroth, and rose away,
      Saies, 'Nay, that cannot bee!
    For that I will keepe for my cheefe chamber,
      Gotten gif that it bee.

24. 'But take thee North Wales and Weschester,
    The countrye all round about,
And rewarded thou shalt bee,
    Of that take thou noe doubt.'

25. Five score knights he made on a day,
    And dubb'd them with his hands;
Rewarded them right worthilye
    With the townes in merry England.

26. And when the fresh knights they were made,
    To battell they buske them bowne
James Douglas he went before,
    And he thought to have wonnen him shoone.

27. But they were mett in a morning of May
    With the comminaltye of litle England;
But there scapèd never a man away,
    Through the might of Christès hand.

28. But all onely Jamès Douglas;
    In Durham in the ffeild
An arrow stroke him in the thye;
    Fast flinges he towards the King.

29. The King looked toward litle Durham,
    Saies, 'All things is not weel!
For James Douglas beares an arrow in his
        thye,
    The head of it is of steele.

30. 'How now, James?' then said the King,
    'How now, how may this bee?
  And where beene all thy merrymen
    That thou tooke hence with thee?'

31. 'But cease, my King,' saies James Douglas,
    'Alive is not left a man!'
  'Now by my faith,' saies the King of Scotts,
    'That gate was evil gone.

32. 'But I'le revenge thy quarrell well,
    And of that thou may be fain;
  For one Scott will beate five Englishmen,
    If they meeten them on the plaine.'

33. 'Now hold your tongue,' saies James Douglas,
    'For in faith that is not soe;
  For one English man is worth five Scotts,
    When they meeten together thoe.

34. 'For they are as eager men to fight
    As a faulcon upon a prey;
  Alas! if ever they winne the vanward,
    There scapes noe man away.'

35. 'O peace thy talking,' said the King,
    'They bee but English knaves,
  But shepards and millers both,
    And priestès with their staves.'

36. The King sent forth one of his heralds of armes
    To vew the Englishmen:
  'Be of good cheere,' the herald said,
    'For against one we be ten.'

37. 'Who leads those lads?' said the King of
        Scotts,
    'Thou herald, tell thou mee:'
  The herald said, 'The Bishop of Durham
    Is captaine of that companye.

38. 'For the Bishop hath spred the King's banner,
    And to battell he buskes him bowne';
  'I sweare by St. Andrewes bones,' saies the
        King,
    'I'll rapp that priest on the crowne!'

39. The King look'd towards litle Durham,
    And that hee well beheld,
  That the Earle Percy was well arm'd,
    With his battell-axe entred the feild.

40. The King look'd again towards litle Durham,
    Four ancyents there saw he;
  There were two standards, six in a valley,
    He cold not see them with his eye.

41. My Lord of Yorke was one of them,
    My Lord of Carlile was the other,
  And my Lord Fitzwilliams,
    The Bishop came with the other.

42. The Bishop of Durham commanded his men,
      And shortlye he them bade,
    That never a man shold goe to fight
      Till he had served his God.

43. Five hundred priests said mass that day
      In Durham in the field,
    And afterwards, as I hard say,
      They bare both spear and shield.

44. The Bishop orders himselfe to fight,
      With his battell-axe in his hand;
    He said, 'This day now I will fight
      As long as I can stand!'

45. 'And soe will I,' sayd my Lord of Carlile,
      'In this faire morning gay';
    'And soe will I,' said my Lord Fitzwilliams,
      'For Mary, that mild may.'

46. Our English archers bent their bowes
      Shortly and anon;
    They shot over the Scottish oast
      And scantly toucht a man.

47. 'Hold downe your hands,' sayd the Bishop of
          Durham,
      'My archers good and true'!
    The second shootè that they shott,
      Full sore the Scots it rue.

48. The Bishop of Durham spoke on hie,
    That both partyes might heare:
  'Be of good cheere, my merrymen all,
    They flyen and changen their cheere!'

49. But as they saidden, see they didden,
    They fell on heapès hie;
  Our Englishmen laid on with their bowes,
    As fast as they might drie.

50. The King of Scotts in a study stood
    Amongst his companye;
  An arrow stoke him thoro' the nose,
    And thoro' his armorye.

51. The King went to a marsh-side
    And light beside his steede;
  He leanèd him downe on his swordhilts,
    To let his nosè bleede.

52. There follow'd him a yeaman of merry
      England,
    His name was John of Coplande:
  'Yeeld thee, traytor!' saies Coplande then,
    'Thy life lies in my hand.'

53. 'How shold I yeeld me,' says the King,
    'And thou art noe gentleman?'—
  'Noe, by my troth,' sayes Copland there,
    'I am but a poore yeaman.

54. 'What art thou better then I, Sir King?
    Tell me if that thou can!
  What art thou better then I, Sir King,
    Now we be but man to man?'

55. The King smote angerly at Copland,
    Angerly in that stonde;
  Then Copeland was a bold yeaman,
    And bore the King to the ground.

56. He sett the King on a palfrey,
    Himselfe upon a steede;
  He tooke him by the bridle-rayne,
    Towards London he can him lead.

57. And when to London that he came,
    The King from Ffrance was come home,
  And there unto the King of Scotts
    He sayd these words anon.—

58. 'How like you my shepards and my millers?
    My priests with shaven crownes?'—
  'By my fayth, they are the sorest fighters
    That ever I mett on the ground.

59. 'There was never a yeaman in merry England
    But was worth a Scottish knight.'—
  'Ay, by my troth,' said King Edward, and
      laughe,
    'For you fought all against the right.'

60. But now the prince of merry England,
    Worthilye under his sheelde,
  Hath taken captive the King of France,
    At Poytiers in the field.

61. The prince did present his father
    With the lovely King of France,
  And forward of his journey he is gone:
    God send us all good chance!

62. Sayd the King of Scots to the King of France,
    'Well met, brother, too soone!
  Christ leeve that I had taken my way
    Unto the court of Roome!

63. 'And soe wold I,' said the King of France,
    'When I came over the streame,
  That I had taken my journey
    Unto Jerusalem!'

64. Thus ends the battell of fair Durham.
    In one morning of May;
  The battells of Cressey and of Poytiers,
    All within one monthes day.

65. Then was wealthe and welfare in merry
      England,
    Solaces, game, and glee,
  And every man loved other well,
    And the King loved good yeomanrye.

66. But God that made the grasse to growe,
       And leaves on greenwoode tree,
    Now save and keepe our noble King,
       And maintaine good yeomanrye!

THE BATTLE OF OTTERBURN

1. IT fell about the Lammas tide
      When husbands win their hay,
   The doughty Douglas bound him to ride
      In England to take a prey.

2. He has chosen the Graemes, and the Lind- ·
         says light,
      And the gallant Gordons gay;
   And the Earl of Fyfe withouten strife,
      He's bound him over Solwày.

3. They come in over Ottercap Hill
      So down by Rodely Cragge;
   Upon Greene Leyton they lighted down
      Styrande many a stagge.

4. And they have brent the dales of Tyne,
      And harryed Bamborowe shire,
   And the Otter Dale they have brent it hale
      And left it a' on fire.

5. Then spake a berne upon the bent,
      Of comfort that was not cold,

And said, 'We have brent Northumberland,
    We have all wealth in hold.

6. 'Now we have harryed all Bamborowe
      shire
    All the wealth in the world have we:
I rede we ryde to Newcastell
    So still and stalworthlye.'

7. Upon the morrow, when it was day,
    The standards shone full bright;
To Newcastell they took the way,
    And thither they came full right.

8. To Newcastell when that they came,
    The Douglas cry'd on hyght:
'Harry Percy, an thou bidest within,
    Come to the field, and fight! —

9. 'For we have brent Northumberland,
    Thy herytage good and right;
And syne my lodging I have ta'en,
    With my brand dubb'd many a knight.'

10. Sir Harry Percy came to the walls
    The Scottish host for to see,
Sayd, 'An thou hast brent Northumber-
      land,
    Full sore it rueth me.

11. If thou hast haryed all Bamborowe shire,
    Thou hast done me great envye;
For this trespasse thou hast me done
    The tone of us shall die.'

12. 'Where shall I bide thee?'sayd the Douglas,
    'Or where wilt thou come to me?'—
'But gae ye up to Otterbourne,
    And wait there dayès three.

13. 'The roe full rekeles there she rins,
    To make the game and glee;
The falcon and the phesant both,
    To fend thy men and thee.

14. 'There may'st thou have thy wealth at will,
    Well lodg'd thou there may'st be:
It shall not be long ere I come thee till,'
    Sayd Sir Harry Percy.

15. 'There shall I bide thee,' sayd the Douglas,
    'By the faith of my bodye.'—
'There shall I come,' said Sir Harry Percy,
    'My troth I plight to thee.'

16. A pipe of wine over the wall,
    He gave them to their pay,
There he made the Douglas drinke,
    And all his host that day.

17. The Douglas turn'd him homeward again,
    And rode withouten stay;
He pyght his standard at Otterbourne
    Upon a Wedensday.

18. And syne he warned his men to go
    To choose their geldings grass;
And he that had no man to send
    His own servant he was.

19. A Scottish knight hoved on the bent
    At watch, I dare well say,
So was he ware of the noble Percy
    In the dawning of the day.

20. He pryck'd to his pavilion door
    As fast as he might run:
'Awaken, Douglas!' cried the knight,
    'For his sake that sits in throne!

21. 'Awaken, Douglas!' cried the knight,
    'For thou mayst wake with wynne!
Yonder have I spied the proud Percy,
    And seven standards with him.'

22. 'Now by my troth,' the Douglas sayd,
    'It is but a faynèd tale!
He durst not look on my broad banner
    Were all England in hail!

23. 'Was I not yesterday at Newcastell
    That stands so fair on Tyne?
For all the men the Percy had
    He could not gar me to dine.'

24. He stepp'd out at his pavilion-door
    To look an it were lease:
'Array you, lordings, one and all!
    For here begins no peace.

25. 'The Earl of Menteith, thou art my eme,
    The vaward I give to thee:
The Earl of Huntley, cante and keen
    Take him to go with thee.

26. 'The Lord of Buchan, in armure bright,
    On the other side he shall be;
Lord Johnstone and Lord Maxwell
    They two shall go with me.

27. 'Swynton, fair fall upon your pride!
    To battle make you bowne.—
Sir Davy Scott, Sir Walter Steward,
    Sir John of Agerstone!'

28. The Percy came before his host,
    He was ever a gentil knight:
Upon the Douglas loud can he cry
    'I will hold that I have hyght.'

29. 'For thou hast brent Northumberland,
      And done me great envye,
   For this trespasse thou hast me done
      The tone of us shall die.'

30. The Douglas answer'd him again
      With great words upon hie,
   And sayd, 'I have twenty against thy one:
      Behold, and thou mayst see!'

31. With that the Percy was grievèd sore,
      Forsooth as I you say:
   He lighted down upon his foot
      And schoote his horse away.

32. Every man saw that he did so,
      That ryal was ever in rowghte:
   Every man schoote his horse him fro
      And lighted him round about.

33. Sir Harry Percy took the field
      Even thus, as I you say;
   Jesus Christe in hevyn on height
      Did help him well that day.

34. But nine thousand, there was no more.—
      The chronicle will not layne —
   Forty thousand of Scots and four
      That day fought them again.

35. But when the battel began to join,
    In haste there came a knight;
    And letters fair forth hath he ta'en,
    And thus he sayd full right:

36. 'My lord your father greets you well,
    With many a noble knight;
    He doth desire you now to bide,
    That he may see this fight.

37. 'The Baron of Graystoke is out of the west
    With a noble companye:
    All they lodge at your father's this night,
    And the battle fayn would they see.'

38. 'For Jesus' love,' sayd Sir Harry Percy,
    'That died for you and me,
    Wend to my lord my father agayn,
    Say thou saw me not with thee.

39. 'My troth is plight to yon Scottish knight,
    — It nede's me not to layne —
    That I should bide him upon this bent,
    And I have his troth agayn.

40. 'And if that I wend off this growende,
    Forsooth, unfoughten away,
    He would call me but a coward knight
    In his land another day.

41. 'Yet had I liefer be rynde and rent,
        — By Mary, that mickle may!—
    Than ever my manhood be reproved
        With a Scot another day.

42. 'Wherefore shoot, archers, for my sake!
        And let sharp arrows flee.
    Minstrels, play up for your waryson!
        And well quit it shall be.

43. 'Every man thynke on his true-love,
        And mark him to the Trinitye:
    For unto God I make mine avowe
        This day will I not flee.'

44. The blodye herte in the Douglas arms
        His standard stood on hie,
    That every man might full wel knowe;
        Bysyde stood starrès three.

45. The white lyon on the English part,
        Forsooth as I you sayn,
    The lucettes and the cressants both
        The Scot fought them again.

46. Upon Seynt Andrewe loud can they crye,
        And thrice they showt on hyght,
    Syne mark'd them on our English men,
        As I have told you right.

47. Seynt George the bryght, Our Ladye's
        knyght,
    To name they were full fayne;
    Our English men they cry'd on hyght,
    And thrice they shot agayne.

48. With that sharp arrows began to flee,
        I tell you in certayne:
    Men of arms began to joyne,
        Many a doughty man was slayne.

49. The Percy and the Douglas met
        That either of other was fayne;
    They swapp'd together while they swet
        With swords of fyne Collayne:

50. Until the blood from their bassonets ran
        As the roke doth in the rayne;
    'Yield thou to me,' sayd the Douglas,
        'Or elles thou shalt be slayne.

51. 'For I see by thy bryght bassonet
        Thou art some man of myght:
    And so I do by thy burnysh'd brand,
        Thou'rt an earl or elles a knyght.'

52. 'By my good faith,' said the noble Percye,
        'Now hast thou rede full ryght;
    Yet will I never yield me to thee,
        While I may stand and fyght.'

53. They swapp'd together, while that they
      swet,
    With swordès sharp and long;
  Each on other so fast they bette,
    Their helms came in pieces down.

54. The Percy was a man of strength,
    I tell you in this stounde:
  He smote the Douglas at the sword's length
    That he fell to the grounde.

55. The Douglas call'd to his little foot-page
    And sayd, 'Run speedilye,
  And fetch my ain dear sister's son,
    Sir Hugh Montgomery.

56. 'My nephew good,' the Douglas sayd,
    'What recks the death of ane?
  Last night I dream'd a dreary dream
    And I ken the day's thy ain.

57. 'My wound is deep: I am fayn to sleep,
    Take thou the vaward of me,
  And hide me by the bracken bush
    Grows on yon lilye-lee.'

58. He has lifted up that noble lord
    With the saut tears in his e'e;
  He has hidden him in the bracken bush
    That his merry men might not see.

59. The standards stood still on eke side;
    With many a grievous groan
  They fought that day, and all the night;
    Many a doughtye man was slone.

60. The morn was clear, the day drew nie,
    — Yet stiffly in stowre they stood;
  Echone hewing another while they might
      drie,
    Till aye ran down the blood.

61. The Percy and Montgomery met
    That either of other was fayn:
  They swappèd swords, and they two met
    Till the blood ran down between.

62. 'Now yield thee, yield thee, Percy,' he said,
    'Or I vow I'le lay thee low!'
  'To whom shall I yield?' said Earl Percy,
    'Now I see it maun be so.'—

63. 'Thou shalt not yield to lord nor loun,
    Nor yet shalt thou to me;
  But yield thee to the bracken bush
    Grows on yon lilye-lee.'—

64. 'I winna yield to a bracken bush,
    Nor yet I will to a brere;
  But I would yield to Earl Douglas,
    Or Montgomery if he was here.'

65. As soon as he knew Montgomery,
       He stuck his sword's point in ground;
    The Montgomery was a courteous knight,
       And quickly took him by the hand.

66. There was slayne upon the Scottès' side,
       For sooth and certaynlye,
    Sir James a Douglas there was slayne,
       That day that he cou'd dye.

67. The Earl of Menteith he was slayne,
       And gryselye groan'd on the groun';
    Sir Davy Scott, Sir Walter Steward,
       Sir John of Agerstone.

68. Sir Charlès Murray in that place
       That never a foot would flee;
    Sir Hew Maxwell, a lord he was,
       With the Douglas did he dee.

69. There was slayne upon the Scottès' side
       For sooth as I you say,
    Of four and fifty thousand Scottes
       Went but eighteen away.

70. There was slayne upon the English side
       For sooth and certaynlye,
     A gentle Knight, Sir John Fitzhughe,
       It was the more pitye.

71. Sir James Hardbotell there was slayne,
          For him their heartes were sore;
      The gentle Lovell there was slayne,
          That the Percy's standard bore.

72. There was slayne upon the English part
          For sooth as I you say,
      Of ninè thousand English men
          Five hundred came away.

•73. The others slayne were in the field;
          Christ keep their souls from woe!
      Seeing there was so fewè friends
          Against so many a foe.

74. Then on the morn they made them bieres
          Of birch and hazell gray:
      Many a widow with weeping teares
          Their makes they fette away.

75. This fray was fought at Otterbourne,
          Between the night and the day;
      Earl Douglas was buried at the bracken
              bush,
          And the Percy led captive away.

76. Now let us all for the Percy pray
          To Jesu most of might,
      To bring his soul to the bliss of heaven,
          For he was a gentle knight.

CHEVY CHASE

Fytte I

1. THE Percy out of Northumberland,
    An avow to God made he
   That he would hunt in the mountains
    Of Cheviot within days three,
   In the maugre of doughty Douglas,
    And all that e'er with him be.

2. The fattest harts in all Cheviot
    He would kill and carry away.—
   'By my faith,' said the doughty Douglas
        again,
    'I will let that hunting if I may!'

3. Then the Percy out of Banborowe came,
    With him a mighty meinye,
   With fifteen hundred archers bold
    Chosen out of shirès three.

4. This began on a Monday at morn,
    In Cheviot the hills so hye;
   The child may rue that is unborn,
    It was the more pitye.

5. The drivers through the woodès went
    All for to raise the deer,
   Bowmen bicker'd upon the bent
    With their broad arrows clear.

6. Then the wild thoro' the woodès went
   On every sidè shear;
   Grayhounds thoro' the grevès glent
   For to kill their deer.

7. This began on Cheviot the hill abune
   Early on a Monenday;
   By that it drew to the hour of noon
   A hundred fat harts dead there lay.

8. They blew a mort upon the bent,
   They 'sembled on sidès shear;
   To the quarry then the Percy went
   To the brittling of the deer.

9. He said, 'It was the Douglas' promise
   This day to meet me here;
   But I wist he would fail, verament!'
   — A great oath the Percy sware.

10. At the last a squire of Northumberland
    Lookèd at his hand full nigh;
    He was ware o' the doughty Douglas
        coming,
    With him a great meinye.

11. Both with speär, bill and brand,—
    'Twas a mighty sight to see;
    Hardier men both of heart nor hand
    Were not in Christiantè.

12. They were twenty hundred spearmen good,
    Withouten any fail:
  They were born along by the water o'
    Tweed
    I' the boun's o' Teviotdale.

13. 'Leave off the brittling of deer,' he said;
    'To your bows look ye take good heed,
  For sith ye were on your mothers born
    Had ye never so mickle need.'

14. The doughty Douglas on a steed
    Rode all his men beforn;
  His armour glitter'd as did a gleed,
    Bolder bairn was never born.

15. 'Tell me whose men ye are,' he says,
    'Or whose men that ye be;
  Who gave you leave in this Cheviot chase
    In spite of mine and of me?'

16. The first man that him answer made
    It was the good Lord Percye:
  'We will not tell thee whose men we are,
    Nor whose men that we be;
  But we will hunt here in this chase
    In the spite of thine and of thee.

17. 'The fattest harts in all Cheviot
    We have kill'd, to carry away.'—

'By my troth,' said the doughty Douglas
    again,
  'The one of us dies this day.

18. 'Yet to kill allè these guiltless men
    Alas, it were great pitye!
  But, Percy, thou art a lord of land,
    I an earl in my countrye —
  Let all our men on a party stand,
    And do battle of thee and me!'

19. 'Christ's curse on his crown,' said the lord
    [Percye,
  'Whosoever thereto says nay!
  By my troth, thou doughty Douglas,' he says,
    'Thou shalt never see that day —

20. —'Neither in England, Scotland nor France,
    Nor for no man of woman born,
  But, that (and fortune be my chance)
    I dare meet him, one man for one.'

21. Then bespake a squire of Northumberland,
    Richard Witherington was his name;
  'It shall never be told in South England
    To King Harry the Fourth for shame.

22. 'I wot you bin great lordès two,
    I am a poor squire of land;
  Yet I'll ne'er see my captain fight on a field
    And stand myself and look on.

But while that I may my weapon wield
    I'll not fail, both heart and hand.'

23. That day, that day, that dreadful day! —
    The first fytte here I find:
An you'll hear any more o' the hunting of
    Cheviot,
    Yet there is more behind.

Fytte II

24. The Englishmen had their bows y-bent,
    Their hearts were good enow;
The first of arrows that they shot off
    Seven score spearmen they slew.

25. Yet bides the Earl Douglas upon the bent,
    A captain good enoghe;
And that was seenè verament,
    For he wrought them both woe and
        wouche.

26. The Douglas parted his host in three,
    Like a chief chieftain of pride;
With surè spears of mighty tree
    They came in on every side;

27. — Throughè our English archery
    Gave many a woond full wide;

Many a doughty they gar'd to dye,
Which gainèd them no pride.

28. The Englishmen let their bowès be,
And pull'd out brands that were bright;
It was a heavy sight to see
Bright swords on basnets light.

29. Thoro' rich mail and manoplie
Many stern they struck down straight;
Many a freyke that was full free
There under foot did light.

30. At last the Douglas and the Percy met,
Like to captains of might and of main;
They swapt together till they both swat
With swordès of fine Milan.

31. These worthy freykès for to fight
Thereto they were full fain,
Till the blood out of their basnets sprent
As ever did hail or rain.

32. 'Yield thee, Percy,' said the Douglas,
'And i' faith I shall thee bring
Where thou shalt have an Earl's wages
Of Jamie our Scottish king.

33. 'Thou shaltè have thy ransom free,
— I hight thee here this thing;

For the manfullest man thou art that e'er
      I conquer'd in field fighting.'

34. But 'Nay', then said the lord Percye,
    'I told it thee beforn
That I would never yielded be
    To man of a woman born.'

35. With that an arrow came hastily
    Forth of a mighty wane;
And it hath stricken the Earl Douglas
    In at the breastè-bane.

36. Thoro' liver and lungès both
    The sharp arròw is gone,
That never after in his life-days
    He spake mo words but one:
'Twas, 'Fight ye, my merry men, whiles ye
       may,
    For my life-days bin gone!'

37. The Percy leanèd on his brand
    And saw the Douglas dee;
He took the dead man by the hand,
    And said, 'Woe is me for thee!

38. 'To have sav'd thy life I'd have parted with
    My lands for yearès three,
For a better man of heart nor of hand
    Was not in the north countrye.'

39. All this there saw a Scottish knight,
     Sir Hugh the Montgomerye:
   When he saw Douglas to the death was
         dight,
     Through a hundred archerye
   He never stint nor he never blint
     Till he came to the lord Percye.

40. He set upon the lord Percỳ
     A dint that was full sore;
   With a surè spear of a mighty tree
     Thro' the body him he bore,
   O' the t'other side that a man might see
     A large cloth-yard and more.

41. An archer of Northumberland
     Saw slain was the lord Percye:
   He bare a bent bow in his hand,
     Was made of a trusty tree.

42. An arrow that was a cloth-yard long
     To the hard steel halèd he,
   A dint that was both sad and sair
     He set on Montgomerye.

43. The dint it was both sad and sair
     That he on Montgomerye set;
   The swan-feathers that his arrow bare
     With his heart-blood they were wet

44. There was never a freykè one foot would flee,
  But still in stoure did stand;
  Hewing on each other, while they might dree,
   With many a baleful brand.

45. This battle began in Cheviot
   An hour before the noon,
  And when the even-song bell was rung
   The battle was not half done.

46. They took their stand on either hand
   By the lee light of the moon;
  Many had no strength for to stand
   In Cheviot the hills abune.

47. Of fifteen hundred archers of England
   Went away but seventy-and-three;
  Of twenty hundred spearmen of Scotland
   But even five-and-fiftỳ.

48. There was slain with the bold Percye
   Sir John of Agerstoune,
  Sir Roger, the hendè Hartley,
   Sir William, the bold Herone.

49. Sir George, the worthy Loumlye,
   A knight of great renown,
  Sir Ralph, the richè Rabye,
   With dints were beaten down.

50. For Witherington my heart was woe
    That ever he slain should be:
    For when both his legs were hewn in two
    Yet he kneel'd and fought on his knee.

51. There was slayn with the doughty Douglas
    Sir Hugh the Montgomerye,
    Sir Davy Lambwell, that worthy was,
    His sister's son was he.

52. Sir Charles a Murray in that place,
    That never a foot would flee:
    Sir Hew Maxwell, a lord he was,
    With the Douglas did he dee.

53. So on the morrow they made them biers
    Of birch and hazel so gray;
    Many widows with weeping tears
    Came to fetch their makes away.

54. Teviotdale may carp of care,
    Northumberland may make moan,
    For two such captains as slain were there
    On the March-parts shall never be none.

55. Word is come to Edinboro',
    To Jamie the Scottish King,
    Earl Douglas, lieutenant of the Marches,
    Lay slain Cheviot within.

56. His hands the King did weal and wring,
    Said, 'Alas! and woe is me!
    Such another captain Scotland within
    I' faith shall never be!'

57. Word is come to lovely London
    To the fourth Harry, our King,
    Lord Percy, lieutenant of the Marches,
    Lay slain Cheviot within.

58. 'God have mercy on his soul' said King
        Harry,
    'Good Lord, if thy will it be!
    I've a hundred captains in England,' he
        said,
    'As good as ever was he:
    But Percy, an I brook my life,
    Thy death well quit shall be.'

59. And as our King made his avow
    Like a noble prince of renown,
    For Percy he did it well perform
    After, on Homble-down;

60. Where six-and-thirty Scottish knights
    On a day were beaten down;
    Glendale glitter'd on their armour bright
    Over castle, tower and town.

61. This was the Hunting of the Cheviot;
    That e'er began this spurn!

Old men, that knowen the ground well,
　　Call it of Otterburn.

62. There was never a time on the Marche-partès
　　　Since the Douglas and Percy met,
　　But 'tis marvel an the red blood run not
　　　As the reane does in the street.

63. Jesu Christ! our balès bete,
　　　And to the bliss us bring!
　　This was the Hunting of the Cheviot:
　　　God send us all good endìng!

WILLIE MACINTOSH

1. 'TURN, Willie Macintosh,
　　　Turn, I bid you;
　　Gin ye burn Auchindown,
　　　Huntly will head you.'—

2. 'Head me or hang me,
　　　That canna fley me;
　　I'll burn Auchindown
　　　Ere the life lea' me.'

3. Coming down Deeside,
　　　In a clear morning,
　　Auchindown was in flame,
　　　Ere the cock-crawing.

4. But coming o'er Cairn Croom,
　　And looking down, man,
　I saw Willie Macintosh
　　Burn Auchindown, man.

5. 'Bonnie Willie Macintosh,
　　Whare left ye your men?'—
　'I left them in the Stapler,
　　But they'll never come hame.'

6. 'Bonny Willie Macintosh,
　　Whare now is your men?'–
　'I left them in the Stapler,
　　Sleeping in their sheen.'

THE BONNIE HOUSE O' AIRLIE

1. IT fell on a day, and a bonnie simmer day,
　　When green grew aits and barley,
　That there fell out a great dispute
　　Between Argyll and Airlie.

2. Argyll has raised an hunder men,
　　An hunder harness'd rarely,
　And he's awa' by the back of Dunkell,
　　To plunder the castle of Airlie.

3. Lady Ogilvie looks o'er her bower-window,
　　And O but she looks warely!

And there she spied the great Argyll,
    Come to plunder the bonnie house of Airlie.

4. 'Come down, come down, my Lady Ogilvie,
    Come down and kiss me fairly.'—
'O I winna kiss the fause Argyll,
    If he shouldna leave a standing stane in Airlie.

5. He hath taken her by the left shoulder,
    Says, 'Dame, where lies thy dowry?'—
'O it's east and west yon wan water side,
    And it's down by the banks of the Airlie.'

6. They hae sought it up, they hae sought it down,
    They hae sought it maist severely,
Till they fand it in the fair plum-tree
    That shines on the bowling-green of Airlie.

7. He hath taken her by the middle sae small,
    And O but she grat sairly!
And laid her down by the bonnie burn-side,
    Till they plunder'd the castle of Airlie.

8. 'Gif my gude lord war here this night,
    As he is with King Charlie,
Neither you, nor ony ither Scottish lord,
    Durst avow to the plundering of Airlie.

9. 'Gif my gude lord war now at hame,
    And he is with his king,

There durst nae a Campbell in a' Argyll
    Set fit on Airlie green.

10. 'Ten bonnie sons I have borne unto him,
    The eleventh ne'er saw his daddy;
But though I had an hunder mair,
    I'd gie them a' to King Charlie!'

JOHNNIE OF COCKERSLEE

1. JOHNNIE rose up in a May morning,
    Call'd for water to wash his hands;
'Gar loose to me the gude gray dogs,
    That are bound wi' iron bands.'

2. When Johnnie's mother gat word o' that,
    Her hands for dule she wrang;
'O Johnnie, for my benison,
    To the greenwood dinna gang!

3. 'Eneugh ye hae o' gude wheat bread,
    And eneugh o' the blude-red wine;
And therefore for nae venison, Johnnie,
    I pray ye, stir frae hame.

4. 'There are Seven For'sters at Hislinton side,
    At Hislinton where they dwell,
And for ae drap o' thy heart's blude
    They wad ride the fords o' hell.'

5. But Johnnie has buskit his gude bend-bow,
    His arrows, ane by ane,
  And he has gane to Durrisdeer
    To ding the dun deer down.

6. He's lookit east, and he's lookit west,
    And a little below the sun;
  And there he spied the dun deer lying
    Aneath a buss o' broom.

7. Johnnie he shot and the dun deer lap,
    And he wounded her on the side;
  But atween the wood and the wan water
    His hounds they laid her pride.

8. And Johnnie has brittled the deer sae well,
    Had out her liver and lungs;
  And wi' these he has feasted his bluidy hounds
    As if they had been Earl's sons.

9. They ate sae much o' the venison,
    And drank sae much o' the blude,
  That Johnnie and his gude gray hounds
    Fell asleep by yonder wood.

10. By there came a silly auld carle,
    An ill death mote he die!
  And he's awa' to Hislinton,
    Where the Seven Foresters did lie

11. 'What news, what news, ye gray-headed carle?
     What news? come tell to me.'—
     'I bring nae news,' said the gray-headed carle,
     'But what these eyes did see.

12. 'High up in Braidislee, low down in Braidislee,
     And under a buss o' scroggs,
     The bonniest childe that ever I saw
     Lay sleeping atween his dogs.

13. 'The sark he had upon his back
     It was o' the holland fine,
     The doublet he had over that
     It was o' the Lincoln twine.

14. 'The buttons that were on his sleeve
     Were o' the gowd sae gude;
     The twa gray dogs he lay atween,
     Their mouths were dyed wi' blude.'

15. Then out and spak' the First Forester,
     The head man owre them a';
     'If this be Johnnie o' Cockerslee
     Nae nearer will we draw.'

16. But up and spak' the Sixth Forester,
     (His sister's son was he,)
     'If this be Johnnie o' Cockerslee,
     We soon shall gar him dee!'

17. The first flight of arrows the Foresters shot,
    They wounded him on the knee;
    And out and spak' the Seventh Forester,
    'The next will gar him dee.'

18. 'O some they count ye well-wight men,
    But I do count ye nane;
    For you might well ha' waken'd me,
    And ask'd gin I wad be ta'en.

19. 'The wildest wolf in a' this wood
    Wad no ha' done sae by me;
    She ha' wet her foot i' the wan water,
    And sprinkled it owre my bree,
    And if that wad not ha' waken'd me,
    Wad ha' gone an' let me be.

20. 'O bows of yew, if ye be true,
    In London where ye were bought;
    And, silver strings, value me sma' things
    Till I get this vengeance wrought!
    And, fingers five, get up belive:
    And Manhood fail me nought!

21. 'Stand stout, stand stout, my noble dogs,
    Stand stout and dinna flee!
    Stand fast, stand fast, my good gray hounds,
    And we will gar them dee!'

22. Johnnie has set his þack to an aik,
    His foot against a stane,

And he has slain the Seven Foresters,
    He has slain them a' but ane.

23. He has broke three ribs in that ane's side,
    But and his collar bane;
He's flung him twa-fald owre his steed,
    Bade him carry the tidings hame . . .

24. 'Is there no a bird in a' this forest
    Will do as mickle for me
As dip its wing in the wan water
    And straik it on my e'e-bree?

25. 'Is there no a bird in a' this forest
    Can sing as I can say,—
Can flee away to my mother's bower
    And tell to fetch Johnnie away?'

26. The starling flew to her window-stane,
    It whistled and it sang;
And aye the owre-word o' the tune
    Was, *Johnnie tarries lang!*

27. They made a rod o' the hazel-bush,
    Another o' the slae-thorn tree,
And mony, mony were the men
    At the fetching our Johnnie.

28. Then out and spak' his auld mother,
    And fast her tears did fa'·

'Ye wadna be warn'd, my son Johnnie,
    Frae the hunting to bide awa'!'

29. Now Johnnie's gude bend-bow is broke,
    And his gude gray dogs are slain;
  And his body lies dead in Durrisdeer,
    And his hunting it is done.

KINMONT WILLIE

1. O HAVE ye na heard o' the fause Sakelde?
    O have ye na heard o' the keen Lord Scroope?
  How they hae ta'en bauld Kinmont Willie,
    On Haribee to hang him up?

2. Had Willie had but twenty men,
    But twenty men as stout as he,
  Fause Sakelde had never the Kinmont ta'en,
    Wi' eight score in his companie.

3. They band his legs beneath the steed,
    They tied his hands behind his back;
  They guarded him, fivesome on each side,
    And they brought him ower the Liddel-rack.

4. They led him thro' the Liddel-rack,
    And also thro' the Carlisle sands;
  They brought him in to Carlisle castell,
    To be at my Lord Scroope's commands.

5. 'My hands are tied, but my tongue is free,
     And whae will dare this deed avow?
   Or answer by the Border law?
       Or answer to the bauld Buccleuch?'—

6. 'Now haud thy tongue, thou rank reiver!
     There's never a Scot shall set thee free:
   Before ye cross my castle yate,
       I trow ye shall take farewell o' me.'

7. 'Fear na ye that, my lord,' quo' Willie:
     'By the faith o' my body, Lord Scroope,' he
         said,
   'I never yet lodged in a hostelrie
     But I paid my lawing before I gaed.'

8. Now word is gane to the bauld Keeper,
     In Branksome Ha', where that he lay,
   That Lord Scroope has ta'en the Kinmont Willie
     Between the hours of night and day.

9. He has ta'en the table wi' his hand,
     He garr'd the red wine spring on hie —
   'Now Christ's curse on my head,' he said,
     'But avengèd of Lord Scroope I'll be!

10. 'O is my basnet a widow's curch?
      Or my lance a wand of the willow-tree?
    Or my arm a ladye's lilye hand,
        That an English lord should lightly me!

11. 'And have they ta'en him, Kinmont Willie,
    Against the truce of Border tide?
And forgotten that the bauld Buccleuch
    Is Keeper here on the Scottish side?

12. 'And have they e'en ta'en him, Kinmont Willie,
    Withouten either dread or fear?
And forgotten that the bauld Buccleuch
    Can back a steed, or shake a spear?

13. 'O were there war between the lands,
    As well I wot that there is nane,
I would slight Carlisle castell high,
    Though it were builded of marble stane.

14. 'I would set that castell in a low,
    And sloken it with English blood!
There's never a man in Cumberland
    Should ken where Carlisle castell stood.

15. 'But since nae war's between the lands,
    And there is peace, and peace should be;
I'll neither harm English lad or lass,
    And yet the Kinmont freed shall be.'

16. He has call'd him forty Marchmen bauld,
    I trow they were of his ain name,
Except Sir Gilbert Elliot, call'd
    The Laird of Stobs, I mean the same.

17. He has call'd him forty Marchmen bauld,
    Were kinsmen to the bauld Buccleuch;
With spur on heel, and splent on spauld,
    And gleuves of green, and feathers blue.

18. There were five and five before them a',
    Wi' hunting-horns and bugles bright:
And five and five came wi' Buccleuch,
    Like Warden's men, array'd for fight.

19. And five and five, like a mason-gang,
    That carried the ladders lang and hie;
And five and five, like broken men;
    And so they reach'd the Woodhouselee.

20. And as we cross'd the Bateable Land,
    When to the English side we held,
The first o' men that we met wi',
    Whae sould it be but fause Sakelde?

21. 'Where be ye gaun, ye hunters keen?'
    Quo' fause Sakelde; 'come tell to me!'—
'We go to hunt an English stag,
    Has trespass'd on the Scots countrie.'

22. 'Where be ye gaun, ye marshal men?'
    Quo' fause Sakelde; 'come tell me true'—
'We go to catch a rank reiver,
    Has broken faith wi' the bauld Buccleuch.'

23. 'Where be ye gaun, ye mason lads,
    Wi' a' your ladders, lang and hie?'—
  'We gang to herry a corbie's nest,
    That wons not far frae Woodhouselee.'—

24. 'Where be ye gaun, ye broken men?'
    Quo' fause Sakelde; 'come tell to me!'—
  Now Dickie of Dryhope led that band,
    And the never a word of lear had he.

25. 'Why trespass ye on the English side?
    Row-footed outlaws, stand!' quo' he;
  The never a word had Dickie to say,
    Sae he thrust the lance through his fause bodie.

26. Then on we held for Carlisle toun,
    And at Staneshaw-bank the Eden we cross'd;
  The water was great and meikle of spate,
    But the never a horse nor man we lost.

27. And when we reach'd the Staneshaw-bank,
    The wind was rising loud and hie;
  And there the Laird gar'd leave our steeds,
    For fear that they should stamp and neigh.

28. And when we left the Staneshaw-bank,
    The wind began fu' loud to blaw;
  But 'twas wind and weet, and fire and sleet,
    When we came beneath the castle wa'.

29. We crept on knees, and held our breath,
    Till we placed the ladders against the wa';
  And sae ready was Buccleuch himsell
    To mount the first before us a'.

30. He has ta'en the watchman by the throat,
    He flung him down upon the lead —
  'Had there not been peace between our lands,
    Upon the other side thou hadst gaed! —

31. 'Now sound out, trumpets!' quo' Buccleuch;
    'Let's waken Lord Scroope right merrilie!'
  Then loud the Warden's trumpet blew —
    O wha dare meddle wi' me?

32. Then speedilie to wark we gaed,
    And raised the slogan ane and a',
  And cut a hole through a sheet of lead,
    And so we wan to the castle ha'.

33. They thought King James and a' his men
    Had won the house wi' bow and spear;
  It was but twenty Scots and ten,
    That put a thousand in sic a stear!

34. Wi' coulters, and wi' forehammers,
    We gar'd the bars bang merrilie,
  Until we came to the inner prison,
    Where Willie o' Kinmont he did lie.

35. And when we cam to the lower prison,
     Where Willie o' Kinmont he did lie —
   'O sleep ye, wake ye, Kinmont Willie,
     Upon the morn that thou's to die?'—

36. 'O I sleep saft, and I wake aft;
     It's lang since sleeping was fley'd frae me!
   Gie my service back to my wife and bairns,
     And a' gude fellows that spier for me.'

37. The Red Rowan has hente him up,
     The starkest man in Teviotdale —
   'Abide, abide now, Red Rowan,
     Till of my Lord Scroope I take farewell.

38. 'Farewell, farewell, my gude Lord Scroope!
     My gude Lord Scroope, farewell!' he cried;
   I'll pay you for my lodging mail,
     When first we meet on the Border side.'—

39. Then shoulder high, with shout and cry,
     We bore him down the ladder lang;
   At every stride Red Rowan made,
     I wot the Kinmont's airns play'd clang!

40. 'O mony a time,' quo' Kinmont Willie,
     I have ridden horse baith wild and wood;
   But a rougher beast than Red Rowan
     I ween my legs have ne'er bestrode.

41. 'And mony a time,' quo' Kinmont Willie,
  'I've prick'd a horse out oure the furs;
 But since the day I back'd a steed,
  I never wore sic cumbrous spurs!'

42. We scarce had won the Staneshaw-bank
  When a' the Carlisle bells were rung,
 And a thousand men on horse and foot
  Cam wi' the keen Lord Scroope along.

43. Buccleuch has turn'd to Eden Water,
  Even where it flow'd frae bank to brim,
 And he has plunged in wi' a' his band,
  And safely swam them through the stream.

44. He turn'd him on the other side,
  And at Lord Scroope his glove flung he;
 'If ye like na my visit in merry England,
  In fair Scotland come visit me!'

45. All sore astonish'd stood Lord Scroope,
  He stood as still as rock of stane;
 He scarcely dared to trew his eyes,
  When through the water they had gane.

46. 'He is either himsell a devil frae hell,
  Or else his mother a witch maun be;
 I wadna have ridden that wan water
  For a' the gowd in Christentie.'

HUGHIE THE GRAEME

1. GUDE Lord Scroope's to the hunting gane,
      He has ridden o'er moss and muir;
   And he has grippit Hughie the Graeme,
      For stealing o' the Bishop's mare.

2. 'Now, good Lord Scroope, this may not be!
      Here hangs a broadsword by my side;
   And if that thou canst conquer me,
      The matter it may soon be tryed.'—

3. 'I ne'er was afraid of a traitor thief;
      Although thy name be Hughie the Graeme,
   I'll make thee repent thee of thy deeds,
      If God but grant me life and time.'—

4. 'Then do your worst now, good Lord Scroope,
      And deal your blows as hard as you can!
   It shall be tried within an hour,
      Which of us two is the better man.'—

5. But as they were dealing their blows so free,
      And both so bloody at the time,
   Over the moss came ten yeomen so tall,
      All for to take brave Hughie the Graeme.

6. Then they hae grippit Hughie the Graeme,
      And brought him up through Carlisle town:

The lasses and lads stood on the walls,
 Crying, 'Hughie the Graeme, thou'se ne'er
  gae down!'

7. Then they hae chosen a jury of men,
 The best that were in Carlisle town;
And twelve of them cried out at once,
 'Hughie the Graeme, thou must gae down!'

8. Then up bespak him gude Lord Hume
 As he sat by the judge's knee;
'Twenty white owsen, my gude lord,
 If you'll grant Hughie the Graeme to me.'—

9. 'O no, O no, my gude Lord Hume!
 For sooth and sae it mauna be;
For, were there but three Graemes of the name,
 They suld be hangèd a' for me.'—

10. 'Twas up and spake the gude Lady Hume,
 As she sat by the judge's knee;
'A peck of white pennies, my gude lord judge,
 If you'll grant Hughie the Graeme to me!'—

11. O no, O no, my gude Lady Hume,
 For sooth and so it mist na be;
Were he but the one Graeme of the name,
 He suld be hangèd high for me.'—

12. 'If I be guilty,' said Hughie the Graeme,
 'Of me my friends shall have small talk';

And he's loupèd fifteen feet and three,
　Though his hands they were tied behind his
　　back.

13. He lookèd over his left shoulder,
　　And for to see what he might see;
There was he aware of his auld father,
　　Came tearing his hair most piteouslie.

14. 'O hald your tongue, my father,' he says,
　　'And see that ye dinna weep for me!
For they may ravish me o' my life,
　　But they canna banish me fro' Heaven hie.

15. 'Here, Johnie Armstrang, take thou my sword,
　　That is made o' the metal sae fine;
And when thou comest to the English side,
　　Remember the death of Hughie the Graeme.'

THE DEATH OF PARCY REED

1. GOD send the land deliverance
　　Frae every reaving, riding Scot;
We'll sune hae neither cow nor ewe,
　　We'll sune hae neither staig nor stot.

2. The outlaws come frae Liddesdale,
　　They herry Redesdale far and near;

The rich man's gelding it maun gang,
   They canna pass the puir man's mare.

3. Sure it were weel, had ilka thief
   Around his neck a halter strang;
And curses heavy may they light
   On traitors vile oursels amang!

4. Now Parcy Reed has Crosier taen,
   He has delivered him to the law;
But Crosier says he'll do waur than that,
   He'll make the tower o' Troughend fa'.

5. And Crosier says he will do waur,
   He will do waur if waur can be;
He'll make the bairns a' fatherless,
   And then, the land it may lie lee.

6. 'To the hunting, ho!' cried Parcy Reed,
   'The morning sun is on the dew;
The cauler breeze frae off the fells
   Will lead the dogs to the quarry true.

7. 'To the hunting, ho!' cried Parcy Reed,
   And to the hunting he has gane;
And the three fause Ha's o' Girsonsfield
   Alang wi' him he has them taen.

8. They hunted high, they hunted low,
   By heathery hill and birken shaw;

They raised a buck on Rooken Edge,
    And blew the mort at fair Ealylawe.

9. They hunted high, they hunted low,
    They made the echoes ring amain;
  With music sweet o' horn and hound,
    They merry made fair Redesdale glen.

10. They hunted high, they hunted low,
    They hunted up, they hunted down,
  Until the day was past the prime,
    And it grew late in the afternoon.

11. They hunted high in Batinghope,
    When as the sun was sinking low;
  Says Parcy then, 'Ca' off the dogs,
    We'll bait our steeds and homeward go.'

12. They lighted high in Batinghope,
    Atween the brown and benty ground;
  They had but rested a little while
    Till Parcy Reed was sleeping sound.

13. There's nane may lean on a rotten staff,
    But him that risks to get a fa';
  There's nane may in a traitor trust,
    And traitors black were every Ha'.

14. They've stown the bridle off his steed,
    And they've put water in his lang gun;

They've fixed his sword within the sheath
    That out again it winna come.

15. 'Awaken ye, waken ye, Parcy Reed,
    Or by your enemies be ta'en!
For yonder are the five Crosiers
    A-coming owre the Hingin-stane!'—

16. 'If they be five, and we be four,
    Sae that ye stand alang wi' me,
Then every man ye will take one,
    And only leave but two to me:
We will them meet as brave men ought,
    And make them either fight or flee.'—

17. 'We mayna stand, we canna stand,
    We daurna stand alang wi' thee;
The Crosiers haud thee at a feud,
    And they wad kill baith thee and we.'—

18. 'O turn thee, turn thee, Johnie Ha',
    O turn thee, man, and fight wi' me;
When ye come to Troughend again,
    My gude black naig I will gie thee;
He cost full twenty pound o' gowd,
    Atween my brother·John and me.'—

19. 'I mayna turn, I canna turn,
    I daurna turn and fight wi' thee;
The Crosiers haud thee at a feud,
    And they wad kill baith thee and me.'—

20. 'O turn thee, turn thee, Willie Ha',
    O turn thee, man, and fight wi' me;
    When ye come to Troughend again,
    A yoke o' owsen I'll gie thee '—

21. 'I mayna turn, I canna turn,
    I daurna turn and fight wi' thee;
    The Crosiers haud thee at a feud,
    And they wad kill baith thee and me.'—

22. 'O turn thee, turn thee, Tommy Ha',
    O turn now, man, and fight wi' me;
    If ever we come to Troughend again,
    My daughter Jean I'll gie to thee.'—

23. 'I mayna turn, I canna turn,
    I daurna turn and fight wi' thee;
    The Crosiers haud thee at a feud,
    And they wad kill baith thee and me.'—

24. 'O shame upon ye, traitors a'!
    I wish your hames ye may never see;
    Ye've stown the bridle off my naig,
    And I can neither fight nor flee.

25. 'Ye've stown the bridle off my naig,
    And ye've put water i' my lang gun;
    Ye've fixed my sword within the sheath
    That out again it winna come.'

26. He had but time to cross himsel',
    A prayer he hadna time to say,
    Till round him came the Crosiers keen,
    All riding graith'd and in array.

27. 'Weel met, weel met, now, Parcy Reed,
    Thou art the very man we sought;
    Owre lang hae we been in your debt,
    Now will we pay you as we ought.

28. 'We'll pay thee at the nearest tree,
    Where we shall hang thee like a hound.'—
    Brave Parcy rais'd his fankit sword,
    And fell'd the foremost to the ground.

29. Alake, and wae for Parcy Reed!
    Alake, he was an unarmed man!
    Four weapons pierced him all at once,
    As they assail'd him there and than.

30. They fell upon him all at once,
    They mangled him most cruellie;
    The slightest wound might caused his deid,
    And they hae gi'en him thirty-three;
    They hackit off his hands and feet,
    And left him lying on the lee.

31. 'Now, Parcy Reed, we've paid our debt,
    Ye canna weel dispute the tale,'
    The Crosiers said, and off they rade;
    They rade the airt o' Liddesdale.

32. It was the hour o' gloaming gray,
    When herds come in frae fauld and pen;
    A herd he saw a huntsman lie,
    Says he, 'Can this be Laird Troughen'?'—

33. 'There's some will ca' me Parcy Reed,
    And some will ca' me Laird Troughen';
    It's little matter what they ca' me,
    My faes hae made me ill to ken.

34. 'There's some will ca' me Parcy Reed,
    And speak my praise in tower and town;
    It's little matter what they do now,
    My life-blood rudds the heather brown.

35. 'There's some will ca' me Parcy Reed,
    And a' my virtues say and sing;
    I would much rather have just now
    A draught o' water frae the spring.'

36. The herd flung aff his clouted shoon
    And to the nearest fountain ran;
    He made his bonnet serve a cup,
    And wan the blessing o' the dying man.

37. 'Now, honest herd, ye maun do mair,
    Ye maun do mair, as I you tell;
    Ye maun bear tidings to Troughend,
    And bear likewise my last farewell.

38. 'A farewell to my wedded wife,
    A farewell to my brother John,
Wha sits into the Troughend tower
    Wi' heart as black as any stone.

39. 'A farewell to my daughter Jean,
    A farewell to my young sons five;
Had they been at their father's hand,
    I had this night been man alive.

40. 'A farewell to my followers a',
    And a' my neighbours gude at need;
Bid them think how the treacherous Ha's
    Betrayed the life o' Parcy Reed.

41. 'The laird o' Clennel bears my bow,
    The laird o' Brandon bears my brand;
Whene'er they ride i' the Border-side,
    They'll mind the fate o' the laird Troughend.'

THE DOWIE HOUMS OF YARROW

1. LATE at een, drinkin' the wine,
    And ere they paid the lawin',
  They set a combat them between,
    To fight it in the dawin'.

2. 'O stay at hame, my noble lord!
    O stay at hame, my marrow!

My cruel brother will you betray,
    On the dowie houms o' Yarrow.'—

3. 'O fare ye weel, my lady gay!
        O fare ye weel, my Sarah!
    For I maun gae, tho' I ne'er return
        Frae the dowie banks o' Yarrow.'

4. She kiss'd his cheek, she kamed his hair,
        As she had done before, O;
    She belted on his noble brand,
        An' he's awa to Yarrow.

5. O he's gane up yon high, high hill —
        I wat he gaed wi' sorrow —
    An' in a den spied nine arm'd men,
        I' the dowie houms o' Yarrow.

6. 'O are ye come to drink the wine,
        As ye hae doon before, O?
    Or are ye come to wield the brand,
        On the dowie houms o' Yarrow?'—

7. 'I am no come to drink the wine,
        As I hae done before, O,
    But I am come to wield the brand,
        On the dowie houms o' Yarrow.'

8. Four he hurt an' five he slew,
        On the dowie houms o' Yarrow,

Till that stubborn knight came him,
        behind,
    An' ran his body thorrow.

9. 'Gae hame, gae hame, good brother John,
        An' tell your sister Sarah
    To come an' lift her noble lord,
        Who's sleepin' sound on Yarrow.'

10. 'Yestreen I dream'd a dolefu' dream;
        I ken'd there wad be sorrow;
    I dream'd I pu'd the heather green,
        On the dowie banks o' Yarrow.'

11. She gaed up yon high, high hill —
        I wat she gaed wi' sorrow —
    An' in a den spied nine dead men,
        On the dowie houms o' Yarrow.

12. She kiss'd his cheek, she kamed his hair,
        As oft she did before, O;
    She drank the red blood frae him ran,
        On the dowie houms o' Yarrow.

13. 'O haud your tongue, my douchter dear,
        For what needs a' this sorrow?
    I'll wed you on a better lord
        Than him you lost on Yarrow.'—

14. 'O haud your tongue, my father dear,
        An' dinna grieve your Sarah;

A better lord was never born
  Than him I lost on Yarrow.

15. 'Tak hame your ousen, tak hame your
      'kye,
  For they hae bred our sorrow;
I wiss that they had a' gane mad
  Whan they cam' first to Yarrow.'

HELEN OF KIRCONNELL

1. I WISH I were where Helen lies,
  Night and day on me she cries;
  O that I were where Helen lies,
    On fair Kirconnell lea!

2. Curst be the heart that thought the thought
  And curst the hand that fired the shot,
  When in my arms burd Helen dropt,
    And died to succour me!

3. O think na ye my heart was sair,
  When my Love dropp'd and spak nae mair!
  There did she swoon wi' meikle care,
    On fair Kirconnell lea.

4. As I went down the water side,
  None but my foe to be my guide,
  None but my foe to be my guide,
    On fair Kirconnell lea;

5. I lighted down my sword to draw,
   I hackèd him in pieces sma',
   I hackèd him in pieces sma',
       For her sake that died for me.

6. O Helen fair, beyond compare!
   I'll mak a garland o' thy hair,
   Shall bind my heart for evermair,
       Until the day I dee!

7. O that I were where Helen lies!
   Night and day on me she cries;
   Out of my bed she bids me rise,
       Says, 'Haste, and come to me!'

8. O Helen fair! O Helen chaste!
   If I were with thee, I'd be blest,
   Where thou lies low and taks thy rest,
       On fair Kirconnell lea.

9. I wish my grave were growing green,
   A winding-sheet drawn owre my een,
   And I in Helen's arms lying,
       On fair Kirconnell lea.

10. I wish I were where Helen lies!
    Night and day on me she cries;
    And I am weary of the skies,
        For her sake that died for me.

THE LAMENT OF THE BORDER WIDOW

1. MY love he built me a bonny bower,
   And clad it a' wi' lilye flour;
   A brawer bower ye ne'er did see,
   Than my true love he built for me.

2. There came a man, by middle day,
   He spied his sport, and went away;
   And brought the King that very night,
   Who brake my bower, and slew my knight.

3. He slew my knight, to me sae dear;
   He slew my knight, and poin'd his gear;
   My servants all for life did flee,
   And left me in extremitie.

4. I sew'd his sheet, making my mane;
   I watch'd the corpse, myself alane;
   I watch'd his body, night and day;
   No living creature came that way.

5. I took his body on my back,
   And whiles I gaed, and whiles I sat;
   I digg'd a grave, and laid him in,
   And happ'd him with the sod sae green.

6. But think na ye my heart was sair,
   When I laid the moul' on his yellow hair;
   O think na ye my heart was wae,
   When I turn'd about, away to gae?

7. Nae living man I'll love again,
    Since that my lovely knight is slain;
    Wi' ae lock of his yellow hair
    I'll chain my heart for evermair.

WALY, WALY

1. O WALY, waly, up the bank,
    O waly, waly, down the brae,
    And waly, waly, yon burn-side,
        Where I and my love were wont to gae!
    I lean'd my back unto an aik,
        I thocht it was a trustie tree,
    But first it bow'd and syne it brak',—
        Sae my true love did lichtlie me.

2. O waly, waly, but love be bonnie
        A little time while it is new!
    But when it's auld it waxeth cauld,
        And fadeth awa' like the morning dew.
    O wherefore should I busk my heid,
        Or wherefore should I kame my hair?
    For my true love has me forsook,
        And says he'll never lo'e me mair.

3. Noo Arthur's Seat sall be my bed,
        The sheets sall ne'er be press'd by me;
    Saint Anton's well sall be my drink;
        Since my true love's forsaken me.

Martinmas wind, when wilt thou blaw,
And shake the green leaves off the tree?
O gentle death, when wilt thou come?
For of my life I am wearie.

4. 'Tis not the frost that freezes fell,
Nor blawing snaw's inclemencie,
'Tis not sie cauld that makes me cry;
But my love's heart grown cauld to me.
When we cam' in by Glasgow town,
We were a comely sicht to see;
My love was clad in the black velvet,
An' I mysel' in cramasie.

5. But had I wist before I kiss'd
That love had been so ill to win,
I'd lock'd my heart in a case o' goud,
And pinned it wi' a siller pin.
Oh, oh! if my young babe were born,
And set upon the nurse's knee;
And I mysel' were dead and gane,
And the green grass growing over me!

BOOK VI

LADY ALICE

1. LADY ALICE was sitting in her bower-window,
   Mending her midnight quoif,
   And there she saw as fine a corpse
   As ever she saw in her life.

2. 'What bear ye, what bear ye, ye six men tall?
   What bear ye on your shoulders?'—
   'We bear the corpse of Giles Collins,
   An old and true lover of yours.'—

3. 'O lay him down gently, ye six men tall,
   All on the grass so green,
   And to-morrow, when the sun goes down,
   Lady Alice a corpse shall be seen.

4. 'And bury me in Saint Mary's church,
   All for my love so true,
   And make me a garland of marjoram,
   And of lemon-thyme, and rue.'

5. Giles Collins was buried all in the east,
   Lady Alice all in the west,
   And the roses that grew on Giles Collins's
   grave,
   They reached Lady Alice's breast.

6. The priest of the parish he chanced to pass,
   And he sever'd those roses in twain;
Sure never were seen such true lovers before,
   Nor e'er will there be again.

LORD LOVEL

1. LORD LOVEL he stood at his castle-gate,
   Combing his milk-white steed,
When up came Lady Nancy Belle,
   To wish her lover good speed.

2. 'Where are you going, Lord Lovel?' she said,
   'Oh where are you going?' said she.
'I'm going, my Lady Nancy Belle,
   Strange countries for to see.'

3. 'When will you be back, Lord Lovel?' she said,
   'Oh when will you come back?' said she.
'In a year, or two, or three at the most,
   I'll return to my fair Nancy.'

4. But he had not been gone a year and a day,
   Strange countries for to see,
When languishing thoughts came into his head,
   Lady Nancy Belle he would go see.

5. So he rode, and he rode, on his milk-white steed,
   Till he came to London town,

And there he heard St. Pancras' bells,
  And the people all mourning round.

6. 'Oh what is the matter?' Lord Lovel he said.
    'Oh what is the matter?' said he;
  'A lord's lady is dead,' a woman replied,
    'And some call her Lady Nancỳ.'

7. So he order'd the grave to be open'd wide,
    And the shroud he turnèd down,
  And there he kiss'd her clay-cold lips,
    Till the tears came trickling down.

8. Lady Nancy she died, as it might be, today,
    Lord Lovel he died as tomorrow;
  Lady Nancy she died out of pure, pure grief,
    Lord Lovel he died out of sorrow.

9. Lady Nancy was laid in St. Pancras' Church,
    Lord Lovel was laid in the choir;
  And out of her bosom there grew a red rose,
    And out of her lover's a briar.

10. They grew, and they grew, to the church-
      steeple top,
    And then they could grow no higher;
  So there they entwined in a true-lovers' knot,
    For all lovers true to admire.

BARBARA ALLEN'S CRUELTY

1. In Scarlet town, where I was born,
   There was a fair maid dwellin',
   Made every youth cry *Well-a-way!*
   Her name was Barbara Allen.

2. All in the merry month of May,
   When green buds they were swellin',
   Young Jemmy Grove on his death-bed lay,
   For love of Barbara Allen.

3. He sent his man in to her then,
   To the town where she was dwellin',
   'O haste and come to my master dear,
   If your name be Barbara Allen.'

4. So slowly, slowly rase she up,
   And slowly she came nigh him,
   And when she drew the curtain by —
   'Young man, I think you're dyin'.'

5. 'O it's I am sick and very very sick,
   And it's all for Barbara Allen.'—
   'O the better for me ye'se never be,
   Tho' your heart's blood were a-spillin'!

6. 'O dinna ye mind, young man,' says she,
   'When the red wine ye were fillin',
   That ye made the healths go round and round,
   And slighted Barbara Allen?'

7. He turn'd his face unto the wall,
　　And death was with him dealin':
'Adieu, adieu, my dear friends all,
　　And be kind to Barbara Allen!'

8. As she was walking o'er the fields,
　　She heard the dead-bell knellin';
And every jow the dead-bell gave
　　Cried 'Woe to Barbara Allen.'

9. 'O mother, mother, make my bed,
　　O make it saft and narrow:
My love has died for me to-day,
　　I'll die for him to-morrow.

10. 'Farewell,' she said, 'ye virgins all,
　　And shun the fault I fell in:
Henceforth take warning by the fall
　　Of cruel Barbara Allen.'

THE GARDENER

1. THE gardener stands in his bower-door,
　　With a primrose in his hand,
And by there came a leal maiden
　　As jimp as a willow wand.

2. 'O lady, can you fancy me,
　　For to be my bride?

Ye'se get a' the flowers in my garden
    To be to you a weed.

3. 'The lily white sall be your smock
        Becomes your body best;
    Your head sall be busk'd wi' gillyflower
        And the primrose in your breast.

4. 'Your gown sall be the sweet-william,
        Your coat the camovine,
    Your apron a' the salluds neat
        That taste baith sweet and fine.

5. 'Your stockings sall be o' the braid kail-blade,
        That is baith braid and lang;
    And narrow, narrow at the cute,
        And braid, braid at the brawn.

6. 'Your gloves sall be the marigold,
        All glittering to your hand,
    Well spread o'er wi' the blue blaewort
        That grows amang corn-land.'—

7. 'O fare ye well, young man,' she says,
        'Farewell, and I bid adieu;
    If you can fancy me,' she says,
        'O I cannot fancy you.

8. 'Sin ye've provided a weed for me
        Amang the summer flowers,

Then I'se provide anither for you
  Amang the winter showers.—

9. 'The new-fa'n snaw to be your smock
  Becomes your body best;
  An' your head sall be wound wi' the eastern
      wind,
    An' the cauld rain on your breast.'

THE LOWLANDS O' HOLLAND

1. 'My love has built a bonny ship, and set her on
      the sea,
  With seven score good mariners to bear her com-
      panỳ;
  There's three score is sunk, and three score dead
      at sea,
  And the Lowlands o' Holland has twin'd my love
      and me.

2. 'My love he built another ship, and set her on the
      main,
  And nane but twenty mariners for to bring her
      hame;
  But the weary wind began to rise, and the sea
      began to rout,
  My love then and his bonny ship turn'd wither-
      shins about.

3. 'Then shall neither coif come on my head nor
    comb come in my hair;
  Then shall neither coal nor candle-light shine in
    my bower mair;
  Nor will I love another one until the day I die,
  Sin' the Lowlands o' Holland has twin'd my love
    and me.'—

4. 'O haud your tongue, my daughter dear, be still
    and be content;
  There are mair lads in Galloway, ye neen nae sair
    lament.'—
  'O there is none in Gallow, there's none at a' for
    me,
  For I never loved a love but one, and he's drown'd
    in the sea.'

THE BAILIFF'S DAUGHTER OF ISLINGTON

1. THERE was a youth, and a well-belovèd youth,
    And he was an esquire's son,
  He loved the bailiff's daughter dear,
    That lived in Islington.

2. But she was coy, and she would not believe
    That he did love her so,
  No, nor at any time she would
    Any countenance to him show.

3. But when his friends did understand
      His fond and foolish mind,
   They sent him up to fair London,
      An apprentice for to bind.

4. And when he had been seven long years,
      And his love he had not seen;
   'Many a tear have I shed for her sake
      When she little thought of me.'

5. All the maids of Islington
      Went forth to sport and play;
   All but the bailiff's daughter dear;
      She secretly stole away.

6. She put off her gown of gray,
      And put on her puggish attire;
   She's up to fair London gone,
      Her true-love to require.

7. As she went along the road,
      The weather being hot and dry,
   There was she aware of her true-love,
      At length came riding by.

8. She stept to him, as red as any rose,
      And took him by the bridle-ring:
   'I pray you, kind sir, give me one penny,
      To ease my weary limb.'—

9. 'I prithee, sweetheart, canst thou tell me
 Where that thou wast born?'—
'At Islington, kind sir,' said she,
 'Where I have had many a scorn.

10. 'I prithee, sweetheart, canst thou tell me
 Whether thou dost know
The bailiff's daughter of Islington?'—
 'She's dead, sir, long ago.'—

11. 'Then will I sell my goodly steed,
 My saddle and my bow;
I will into some far countrey,
 Where no man doth me know.'—

12. 'O stay, O stay, thou goodly youth!
 She's alive, she is not dead;
Here she standeth by thy side,
 And is ready to be thy bride.'—

13. 'O farewell grief, and welcome joy,
 Ten thousand times and o'er!
For now I have seen my own true-love,
 That I thought I should have seen no more.

THE BLIND BEGGAR'S DAUGHTER
OF BEDNALL-GREEN

1. It was a blind beggar, had long lost his sight,
He had a fair daughter of beauty most bright;
And many a gallant brave suitor had she,
For none was so comely as pretty Bessee.

2. And though she was of favour most faire,
   Yet seeing she was but a poor beggar's heyre,
   Of ancyent housekeepers despisèd was she,
   Whose sons came as suitors to pretty Bessee.

3. Wherefore in great sorrow fair Bessy did say,
   'Good father, and mother, let me go away
   To seek out my fortune, whatever it be.'
   This suit then they granted to pretty Bessee.

4. Then Bessy, that was of beauty so bright,
   All clad in grey russet, and late in the night,
   From father and mother alone parted she;
   Who sighèd and sobbèd for pretty Bessee.

5. She went till she came to Stratford-le-Bow;
   Then knew she not whither, nor which way to go:
   With tears she lamented her hard destinìe,
   So sad and so heavy was pretty Bessee.

6. She kept on her journey until it was day,
   She went unto Rumford along the high way;
   Where at the Queen's Arms entertainèd was she:
   So fair and well favoured was pretty Bessee.

7. She had not been there a month to an end,
   But master and mistress and all was her friend:
   And every brave gallant, that once did her see,
   Was straightway enamour'd of pretty Bessee.

8. Great gifts they did send her of silver and gold,
   And in their songs daily her love was extoll'd;
   Her beauty was blazèd in every degree;
   So fair and so comely was pretty Bessee.

9. The young men of Rumford in her had their joy;
   She showed herself courteous, and modestly coy;
   And at her commandèment still would they be;
   So fair and so comely was pretty Bessee.

10. Four suitors at once unto her did go;
    They cravèd her favour, but still she said 'No;
    I would not wish gentles to marry with me.'—
    Yet ever they honoured pretty Bessee.

11. The first of them was a gallant young knight,
    And he came unto her disguised in the night:
    The second a gentleman of good degree,
    Who wooèd and suèd for pretty Bessee.

12. A merchant of London, whose wealth was not
          small,
    He was the third suitor, and proper withal
    Her master's own son the fourth man must be,
    Who swore he would die for pretty Bessee.

13. 'And, if thou wilt marry with me,' quoth the
          knight,
    'I'll make thee a lady with joy and delight;
    My heart so enthrallèd is by thy beautìe,
    That soon I shall die for pretty Bessee.'

14. The gentleman said, 'Come, marry with me,
    As fine as a lady my Bessy shall be:
    My life is distressèd: O hear me,' quoth he;
    'And grant me thy love, my pretty Bessee.'—

15. 'Let me be thy husband,' the merchant did say,
    'Thou shalt live in London both gallant and gay;
    My ships shall bring home rich jewels for thee,
    And I will for ever love pretty Bessee.'

16. Then Bessy she sighed, and thus she did say,
    'My father and mother I mean to obey;
    First get their good will, and be faithful to me,
    And then you shall marry your pretty Bessee.'

17. To every one this answer she made,
    Wherefore unto her they joyfully said,
    'This thing to fulfil we all do agree;
    But where dwells thy father, my pretty Bessee?'

18. 'My father,' she said, 'is soon to be seen:
    The silly blind beggar of Bednall-green,
    That daily sits begging for charitìe,
    He is the good father of pretty Bessee.

19. 'His marks and his tokens are known very well;
    He always is led with a dog and a bell:
    A silly old man, God knoweth, is he,
    Yet he is the father of pretty Bessee.'

20. 'Nay then,' quoth the merchant, 'thou art not
　　for me!'
　　'Nor,' quoth the innholder, 'my wife thou shalt
　　be.'
　　'I loathe,' said the gentle, 'a beggar's degree,
　　And therefore adieu, my pretty Bessee!'

21. 'Why then,' quoth the knight, 'hap better or
　　worse,
　　I weigh not true love by the weight of the purse,
　　And beauty is beauty in every degree;
　　Then welcome unto me, my pretty Bessee.

22. 'With thee to thy father forthwith I will go.'—
　　'Nay soft,' quoth his kinsmen, ' it must not be
　　so;
　　A poor beggar's daughter no lady shall be,
　　Then take thy adieu of pretty Bessee.'

23. But soon after this, by break of the day
　　The Knight had from Rumford stole Bessy away
　　The young men of Rumford, as thick as might be
　　Rode after to fetch again pretty Bessee.

24. As swift as the wind to ryde they were seen,
　　Until they came near unto Bednall-green;
　　And as the Knight lighted most courteouslìe,
　　They all fought against him for pretty Bessee.

25. But rescue came speedily over the plain,
    Or else the young Knight for his love had been
        slain.
    This fray being ended, then straightway he see
    His kinsmen come railing at pretty Bessee.

26. Then spake the blind beggar, 'Although I be
        poor,
    Yet rail not against my child at my own door:
    Though she be not deckèd in velvet and pearl,
    Yet will I drop angels with you for my girl

27. 'And then, if my gold may better her birth,
    And equal the gold that you lay on the earth,
    Then neither rail nor grudge you to see
    The blind beggar's daughter a lady to be.

28. 'But first you shall promise, and have it well
        known,
    The gold that you dropt shall all be your own.
    With that they replied, 'Contented be we.'
    'Then here's,' quoth the beggar, 'for pretty
        Bessee!'

29. With that an angel he cast on the ground,
    And dropped in angels full three thousand pound
    And oftentimes it was provèd most plain,
    For the gentlemen's one the beggar dropt twain:

30. So that the place, wherein they did sit,
    With gold it was coverèd every whit.
    The gentlemen then, having dropt all their store,
    Said, 'Now, beggar, hold, for we have no more,

31. 'Thou hast fulfilled thy promise aright.'—
    'Then marry,' quoth he, 'my girl to this Knight;
    And here,' added he, 'I will now throw you down
    A hundred pounds more to buy her a gown.'

32. The gentlemen all, that this treasure had seen,
    Admirèd the beggar of Bednall-green:
    And all those, that were her suitors before,
    Their flesh for very anger they tore.

33. Thus was fair Bessy match'd to the Knight,
    And then made a lady in others' despite:
    A fairer lady there never was seen
    Than the blind beggar's daughter of Bednall-
        green.

34. But of their sumptuous marriage and feast,
    What brave lords and knights thither were prest,
    The second fitt shall set forth to your sight
    With marvellous pleasure and wished delight.

PART II

35. Of a blind beggar's daughter most bright,
    That late was betrothed unto a young Knight;
    All the discourse thereof you did see:
    But now comes the wedding of pretty Bessee.

36. Within a gorgeous palace most brave,
    Adornèd with all the cost they could have,
    This wedding was kept most sumptuouslìe,
    And all for the credit of pretty Bessee.

37. All kind of dainties and delicates sweet
    Were bought for the banquet, as it was most
        meet;
    Partridge, and plover, and venison most free,
    Against the brave wedding of pretty Bessee.

38. This marriage through England was spread by
        report,
    So that a great number thereto did resort
    Of nobles and gentles in every degree;
    And all for the fame of pretty Bessee.

39. To church then went this gallant young Knight;
    His bride followed after, an angel most bright,
    With troops of ladies — the like ne'er was seen
    As went with sweet Bessy of Bednall-green.

40. This marriage being solemnized then,
    With musick performed by the skilfullest men,
    The nobles and gentles sat down at that tide,
    Each one admiring the beautiful bride.

41. Now, after the sumptuous dinner was done,
    To talk and to reason a number begun:

They talk'd of the blind beggar's daughter most
    bright,
And what with his daughter he gave to the
    Knight.

42. Then spake the nobles, 'Much marvel have we,
    This jolly blind beggar we cannot here see.'
    'My lords,' quoth the bride, 'my father's so base
    He is loth with his presence these states to dis-
        grace.'—

43. 'The praise of a woman in question to bring,
    Before her own face, were a flattering thing,
    But we think thy father's baseness,' quoth they,
    'Might by thy beauty be clean put away.'

44. They had no sooner these pleasant words spoke,
    But in comes the beggar clad in a silk cloak;
    A fair velvet cap, and a feather had he,
    And now a musician forsooth he would be.

45. He had a dainty lute under his arm,
    He touchèd the strings, which made such a
        charm,
    Says, 'Please you to hear any musick of me,
    I'll sing you a song of pretty Bessee.'

46. With that his lute he twangèd straightway,
    And thereon began most sweetly to play;
    And after that lessons were played two or three,
    He strain'd out this song most delicatelìe.

47. 'A poor beggar's daughter did dwell on a green,
Who for her fairness might well be a queen:
A blithe bonny lass, and a dainty was she,
And many one callèd her pretty Bessee.

48. 'Her father he had no goods, nor no land,
But begg'd for a penny all day with his hand;
And yet to her marriage he gave thousands three
And still he hath somewhat for pretty Bessee.

49. 'And if any one here her birth do disdain,
Her father is ready, with might and with main,
To prove she is come of noble degree:
Therefore never flout at pretty Bessee.'

50. With that the lords and the company round
With hearty laughter were ready to swound;
At last said the lords, 'Full well we may see,
The bride and the beggar's beholden to thee.'

51. On this the bride all blushing did rise,
The pearly drops standing within her fair eyes,
'O pardon my father, grave nobles,' quoth she,
'That through blind affection thus doteth on
    me.'

52. 'If this be thy father,' the nobles did say,
'Well may he be proud of this happy day;
Yet by his countenance well may we see,
His birth and his fortune did never agree:

53. 'And therefore, blind man, we pray thee bewray
    (And look that the truth thou to us do say)
    Thy birth and thy parentage, what it may be;
    For the love that thou bearest to pretty Bessee.'

54. 'Then give me leave, nobles and gentles, each
        one,
    One song more to sing, and then I have done;
    And if that it may not win good report,
    Then do not give me a groat for my sport.

55. 'Sir Simon de Montfort my subject shall be;
    Once chief of all the great barons was he,
    Yet fortune so cruel this lord did abase,
    Now lost and forgotten are he and his race.

56. 'When the barons in arms did King Henry
        oppose,
    Sir Simon de Montfort their leader they chose;
    A leader of courage undaunted was he,
    And ofttimes he made their enemies flee.

57. 'At length in the battle on Evesham plain,
    The barons were routed, and Montfort was slain;
    Most fatal that battle did prove unto thee,
    Though thou wast not born then, my pretty
        Bessee!

58. 'Along with the nobles, that fell at that tide,
    His eldest son Henry, who fought by his side,

Was fell'd by a blow he received in the fight:
A blow that deprived him for ever of sight.

59. 'Among the dead bodies all lifeless he lay,
Till evening drew on of the following day;
When by a young lady discovered was he;
And this was thy mother, my pretty Bessee!

60. 'A baron's fair daughter stept forth in the night
To search for her father, who fell in the fight,
And seeing young Montfort, where gasping he
    lay,
Was movèd with pity, and brought him away

61. 'In secret she nurst him, and swagèd his pain,
While he through the realm was believed to be
    slain:
At length his fair bride she consented to be,
And made him glad father of pretty Bessee.

62. 'And now, lest our foes our lives should betray,
We clothèd ourselves in beggars' array;
Her jewels she sold, and hither came we:
All our comfort and care was our pretty Bessee.

63. 'And here have we livèd in fortune's despite,
Though poor, yet contented with humble delight:
Full forty winters thus have I been
A silly blind beggar of Bednall-green.

64. 'And here, noble lords, is ended the song
Of one that once to your own rank did belong:
And thus have you learnèd a secret from me,
That ne'er had been known, but for pretty
Bessee.'

65. Now when the fair company every one,
Had heard the strange tale in the song he had
shown,
They all were amazèd, as well they might be,
Both at the blind beggar, and pretty Bessee.

66. With that the fair bride they all did embrace,
Saying, 'Sure thou art come of an hon'rable race;
Thy father likewise is of noble degree,
And thou art well worthy a lady to be.'

67. Thus was the feast ended with joy and delight,
A bridegroom most happy then was the young
Knight,
In joy and felicitie long livèd he,
All with his fair lady, the pretty Bessee.

THE LOVING BALLAD OF LORD BATEMAN

A Broadside Version of 'Young Beichan'

1. LORD BATEMAN was a noble lord,
A noble lord of high degree;

He shipp'd himself all aboard of a ship,
　　Some foreign country for to see.

2. He sailèd east, he sailèd west,
　　Until he came to famed Turkey,
　Where he was taken and put to prison,
　　Until his life was quite weary.

3. All in this prison there grew a tree,
　　O there it grew so stout and strong!
　Where he was chain'd all by the middle,
　　Until his life was almost gone.

4. This Turk he had one only daughter,
　　The fairest my two eyes e'er see;
　She stole the keys of her father's prison,
　　And swore Lord Bateman she would let
　　　　go free.

5. O she took him to her father's cellar,
　　And gave to him the best of wine;
　And every health she drank unto him
　　Was,'I wish, Lord Bateman, as you was mine.'

6. 'O have you got houses, have you got land,
　　And does Northumberland belong to thee?
　And what would you give to the fair young lady
　　As out of prison would let you go free?'—

7. 'O I've got houses and I've got land,
　　And half Northumberland belongs to me;

And I will give it all to the fair young lady
　　As out of prison would let me go free.'—

8. 'O in seven long years, I'll make a vow
　　For seven long years, and keep it strong,
That if you'll wed no other woman,
　　O I will wed no other man.'

9. O she took him to her father's harbour,
　　And gave to him a ship of fame,
Saying, 'Farewell, farewell to you, Lord Bate-
　　　　man,
　　I fear I never shall see you again!'

10. Now seven long years is gone and past,
　　And fourteen days, well known to me;
She packèd up all her gay clothing,
　　And swore Lord Bateman she would go see.

11. O when she arrived at Lord Bateman's castle,
　　How boldly then she rang the bell!
'Who's there? who's there?' cries the proud
　　　　young porter,
　　'O come unto me pray quickly tell.'—

12. 'O is this here Lord Bateman's castle,
　　And is his lordship here within?'—
'O yes, O yes,' cries the proud young porter,
　　'He's just now taking his young bride in.'—

13. 'O bid him to send me a slice of bread,
    And a bottle of the very best wine,
  And not forgetting the fair young lady
    As did release him when close confine.'

14. O away and away went this proud young porter
    O away and away and away went he,
  Until he came to Lord Bateman's chamber,
    When he went down on his bended knee.

15. 'What news, what news, my proud young porter?
    What news, what news? Come tell to me.'—
  'O there is the fairest young lady
    As ever my two eyes did see.

16. 'She has got rings on every finger,
    And on one finger she has got three;
  With as much gay gold about her middle
    As would buy half Northumberlee.

17. 'O she bids you to send her a slice of bread,
    And a bottle of the very best wine,
  And not forgetting the fair young lady
    As did release you when close confine.'

18. Lord Bateman then in passion flew,
    And broke his sword in splinters three,
  Saying, 'I will give half of my father's land,
    If so be as Sophia has crossed the sea.'

19. Then up and spoke this young bride's mother,
     Who never was heard to speak so free;
     Saying, 'You'll not forget my only daughter,
       If so be as Sophia has crossed the sea.'—

20. 'O it's true I made a bride of your daughter,
     But she's neither the better nor the worse for
         me;
     She came to me with a horse and saddle,
       But she may go home in a coach and three.'

21. Lord Bateman then prepared another marriage,
     With both their hearts so full of glee,
     Saying, 'I'll roam no more to foreign countries,
       Now that Sophia has crossed the sea.'

THE OLD CLOAK

1.   THIS winter's weather it waxeth cold,
           And frost it freezeth on every hill,
         And Boreas blows his blast so bold
           That all our cattle are like to spill.
         Bell, my wife, she loves no strife;
           She said unto me quietlye,
         'Rise up, and save cow Crumbock's life!
           Man, put thine old cloak about thee!'

2. *He.* O Bell my wife, why dost thou flyte?
         Thou kens my cloak is very thin:

It is so bare and over worn,
  A crickè thereon cannot renn.
Then I'll no longer borrow nor lend;
  For once I'll new apparell'd be;
To-morrow I'll to town and spend;
  For I'll have a new cloak about me.

3. *She.* Cow Crumbock is a very good cow:
  She has been always true to the pail;
She has help'd us to butter and cheese, I
    trow,
  And other things she will not fail.
I would be loth to see her pine.
  Good husband, counsel take of me:
It is not for us to go so fine —
  Man, take thine old cloak about thee!

4. *He.* My cloak it was a very good cloak,
  It hath been always true to the wear;
But now it is not worth a groat:
  I have had it four and forty year'.
Sometime it was of cloth in grain:
  'Tis now but a sigh clout, as you may
    see:
It will neither hold out wind nor rain;
  And I'll have a new cloak about me.

5. *She.* It is four and forty years ago
  Sine the one of us the other did ken;

And we have had, betwixt us two,
  Of children either nine or ten:
We have brought them up to women and
    men:
  In the fear of God I trow they be:
And why wilt thou thyself misken?
  Man, take thine old cloak about thee!

6. *He.* O Bell my wife, why dost thou flyte?
  Now is now, and then was then:
Seek now all the world throughout,
  Thou kens not clowns from gentlemen:
They are clad in black, green, yellow and
    blue,
  So far above their own degree.
Once in my life I'll take a view;
  For I'll have a new cloak about me.

7. *She.* King Stephen was a worthy peer;
  His breeches cost him but a crown;
He held them sixpence all too dear,
  Therefore he called the tailor 'lown.'
He was a king and wore the crown,
  And thou'se but of a low degree:
It's pride that puts this country down:
  Man, take thy old cloak about thee!

8. *He.* Bell my wife, she loves not strife,
  Yet she will lead me, if she can:

And to maintain an easy life
    I oft must yield, though I'm good-man.
It's not for a man with a woman to threap,
    Unless he first give o'er the plea:
As we began, so will we keep,
    And I'll take my old cloak about me.

GET UP AND BAR THE DOOR

1. It fell about the Martinmas time,
    And a gay time it was then,
When our goodwife got puddings to make,
    And she's boil'd them in the pan.

2. The wind sae cauld blew south and north,
    And blew into the floor;
Quoth our goodman to our goodwife,
    'Gae out and bar the door.'—

3. 'My hand is in my hussyfskap,
    Goodman, as ye may see;
An' it shou'dna be barr'd this hundred year,
    It's no be barr'd for me.'

4. They made a paction 'tween them twa,
    They made it firm and sure,
That the first word whae'er shou'd speak,
    Shou'd rise and bar the door.

5. Then by there came two gentlemen,
      At twelve o'clock at night,
   And they could neither see house nor hall,
      Nor coal nor candle-light.

6. 'Now whether is this a rich man's house,
      Or whether is it a poor?'
   But ne'er a word wad ane o' them speak,
      For barring of the door.

7. And first they ate the white puddings,
      And then they ate the black.
   Tho' muckle thought the goodwife to hersel'
      Yet ne'er a word she spake.

8. Then said the one unto the other,
      'Here, man, tak ye my knife;
   Do ye tak aff the auld man's beard,
      And I'll kiss the goodwife.'—

9. 'But there's nae water in the house,
      And what shall we do than?'—
   'What ails ye at the pudding-broo,
      That boils into the pan?'

10. O up then started our goodman,
      An angry man was he:
    'Will ye kiss my wife before my een,
      And sca'd me wi' pudding-bree?'

11. Then up and started our goodwife,
      Gied three skips on the floor:
      'Goodman, you've spoken the foremost word!
      Get up and bar the door.'

KING JOHN AND THE ABBOT OF CANTERBURY

1. An ancient story I'll tell you anon
    Of a notable prince, that was callèd King John;
    And he rulèd England with maine and with
          might,
    For he did great wrong, and maintein'd little
          right.

2. And I'll tell you a story, a story so merrye,
    Concerning the Abbot of Canterburye;
    How, for his house-keeping and high renowne,
    They rode poste for him to fair London towne.

3. An hundred men, the King did heare say,
    The Abbot kept in his house every day;
    And fifty golde chaynes, without any doubt,
    In velvet coates waited the Abbot about.

4. 'How now, Father Abbot, I heare it of thee
    Thou keepest a farre better house than mee,
    And for thy house-keeping and high renowne,
    I feare thou work'st treason against my crown.'

5. 'My liege,' quo' the Abbot, 'I would it were
      knowne,
  I never spend nothing, but what is my owne;
  And I trust your Grace will doe me no deere
  For spending of my owne true-gotten geere.'

6. 'Yes, yes, Father Abbot, thy fault it is highe,
  And now for the same thou needest must dye;
  For except thou canst answer me questions three
  Thy head shall be smitten from thy bodìe.

7. 'And first,' quo' the King, 'when I'm in this
      stead,
  With my crowne of golde so faire on my head,
  Among all my liege-men so noble of birthe,
  Thou must tell me to one penny what I am
      worthe.

8. 'Secondlye, tell me without any doubt,
  How soone I may ride the whole worlde about.
  And at the third question thou must not shrinke,
  But tell me here truly what I do thinke.'—

9. 'O, these are hard questions for my shallow witt,
  Nor I cannot answer your Grace as yet:
  But if you will give me but three weekes space,
  I'll do my endeavour to answer your Grace.'

10. 'Now three weekes space to thee will I give,
  And that is the longest time thou hast to live;
  For if thou dost not answer my questions three,
  Thy lands and thy livings are forfeit to mee.'

11. Away rode the Abbot all sad at that word,
    And he rode to Cambridge, and Oxenford;
    But never a doctor there was so wise,
    That could with his learning an answer devise.

12. Then home rode the Abbot of comfort so cold,
    And he mett with his shepheard a-going to fold:
    'How now, my lord Abbot, you are welcome
       home;
    What newes do you bring us from good King
       John?'—

13. 'Sad newes, sad newes, shepheard, I must give;
    That I have but three days more to live:
    For if I do not answer him questions three,
    My head will be smitten from my bodìe.

14. 'The first is to tell him there in that stead,
    With his crowne of golde so fair on his head,
    Among all his liege-men so noble of birthe,
    To within one penny of what he is worthe.

15. 'The seconde, to tell him, without any doubt,
    How soone he may ride this whole worlde about:
    And at the third question I must not shrinke,
    But tell him there truly what he does thinke.'—

16. 'Now cheare up, sire Abbot, did you never hear
       yet,
    That a fool he may learn a wise man witt?

Lend me horse, and serving-men, and your
 apparel,
And I'll ride to London to answere your quarrel.

17. 'Nay frowne not, if it hath bin told unto mee,
 I am like your lordship, as ever may bee:
 And if you will but lend me your gowne,
 There is none shall knowe us at fair London
  towne.'—

18. 'Now horses and serving-men thou shalt have,
 With sumptuous array most gallant and brave;
 With crozier, and miter, and rochet, and cope,
 Fit to appeare 'fore our Father the Pope.'—

19. 'Now welcome, sire Abbot,' the King he did say,
 ''Tis well thou'st come back to keepe thy day;
 For and if thou canst answer my questions three,
 Thy life and thy living both savèd shall bee.

20. 'And first, when thou seest me here in this stead,
 With my crown of golde so fair on my head,
 Among all my liege-men so noble of birthe,
 Tell me to one penny what I am worthe.'—

21. 'For thirty pence our Saviour was sold
 Amonge the false Jewes, as I have bin told;
 And twenty-nine is the worthe of thee,
 For I thinke thou art one penny worser than hee.'

22. The King he laughed, and swore by St. Bittel,
    'I did not thinke I had been worthe so littel!
    — Now secondly tell me, without any doubt,
    How soone I may ride this whole world about.'—

23. 'You must rise with the sun, and ride with the
            same,
    Until the next morning he riseth againe;
    And then your Grace need not make any doubt,
    But in twenty-four hours you'll ride it about.'

24. The King he laughed, and swore by St. Jone,
    'I did not think it could be gone so soone!
    — Now from the third question thou must not
            shrinke,
    But tell me here truly what I do thinke.'—

25. 'Yea, that shall I do, and make your Grace
            merry:
    You thinke I'm the Abbot of Canterburye;
    But I'm his poor shepheard, as plain you may
            see,
    That am come to beg pardon for him and for
            mee.'

26. The King he laughed, and swore by the Masse,
    'I'll make thee Lord Abbot this day in his
            place!'—
    'Now naye, my liege, be not in such speede,
    For alacke I can neither write, ne reade.'—

27. 'Four nobles a weeke, then, I will give thee
    For this merry jest thou hast showne unto mee;
    And tell the old Abbot when thou comest home,
    Thou hast brought him a pardon from good King
        John.'

THE CHILDREN IN THE WOOD

1. Now ponder well, you parents dear,
    These words which I shall write;
  A doleful story you shall hear,
    In time brought forth to light.
  A gentleman of good account
    In Norfolk dwelt of late,
  Who did in honour far surmount
    Most men of his estate.

2. Sore sick he was and like to die,
    No help his life could save;
  His wife by him as sick did lie,
    And both possest one grave.
  No love between these two was lost,
    Each was to other kind;
  In love they lived, in love they died,
    And left two babes behind:

3. The one a fine and pretty boy
    Not passing three years old,
  The other a girl more young than he,
    And framed in beauty's mould.

The father left his little son,
  As plainly did appear,
When he to perfect age should come,
  Three hundred pounds a year;

4. And to his little daughter Jane
    Five hundred pounds in gold,
  To be paid down on marriage-day,
    Which might not be controll'd.
  But if the children chanced to die
    Ere they to age should come,
  Their uncle should possess their wealth;
    For so the will did run.

5. 'Now, brother,' said the dying man,
    'Look to my children dear;
  Be good unto my boy and girl,
    No friends else have they here:
  To God and you I recommend
    My children dear this day;
  But little while be sure we have
    Within this world to stay.

6. 'You must be father and mother both,
    And uncle, all in one;
  God knows what will become of them
    When I am dead and gone.'
  With that bespake their mother dear:
    'O brother kind,' quoth she,

'You are the man must bring our babes
To wealth or misery!

7. 'And if you keep them carefully,
Then God will you reward;
But if you otherwise should deal,
God will your deeds regard.'
With lips as cold as any stone,
They kiss'd their children small:
'God bless you both, my children dear!'
With that the tears did fall.

8. These speeches then their brother spake
To this sick couple there:
'The keeping of your little ones,
Sweet sister, do not fear;
God never prosper me nor mine,
Nor aught else that I have,
If I do wrong your children dear
When you are laid in grave!'

9. The parents being dead and gone,
The children home he takes,
And brings them straight unto his house,
Where much of them he makes.
He had not kept these pretty babes
A twelvemonth and a day,
But, for their wealth, he did devise
To make them both away.

10. He bargain'd with two ruffians strong,
    Which were of furious mood,
    That they should take these children young
    And slay them in a wood.
    He told his wife an artful tale:
    He would the children send
    To be brought up in London town
    With one that was his friend.

11. Away then went those pretty babes,
    Rejoicing at that tide,
    Rejoicing with a merry mind
    They should on cock-horse ride.
    They prate and prattle pleasantly,
    As they ride on the way,
    To those that should their butchers be
    And work their lives' decay:

12. So that the pretty speech they had
    Made Murder's heart relent;
    And they that undertook the deed
    Full sore did now repent.
    Yet one of them, more hard of heart,
    Did vow to do his charge,
    Because the wretch that hirèd him
    Had paid him very large.

13. The other won't agree thereto,
    So here they fall to strife;

With one another they did fight
   About the children's life:
And he that was of mildest mood
   Did slay the other there,
Within an unfrequented wood. —
   The babes did quake for fear!

14. He took the children by the hand,
    Tears standing in their eye,
  And bade them straightway follow him,
    And look they did not cry;
  And two long miles he led them on,
    While they for food complain:
  'Stay here,' quoth he; 'I'll bring you bread
    When I come back again.'

15. These pretty babes, with hand in hand,
    Went wandering up and down;
  But never more could see the man
    Approaching from the town.
  Their pretty lips with blackberries
    Were all besmear'd and dyed;
  And when they saw the darksome night,
    They sat them down and cried.

16. Thus wander'd these poor innocents,
    Till death did end their grief;
  In one another's arms they died,
    As wanting due relief:

No burial this pretty pair
From any man receives,
Till Robin Redbreast piously
Did cover them with leaves.

17. And now the heavy wrath of God
Upon their uncle fell;
Yea, fearful fiends did haunt his house,
His conscience felt an hell:
His barns were fired, his goods consumed,
His lands were barren made,
His cattle died within the field,
And nothing with him stay'd.

18. And in a voyage to Portugal
Two of his sons did die;
And, to conclude, himself was brought
To want and misery:
He pawn'd and mortgaged all his land
Ere seven years came about,
And now at last his wicked act
Did by this means come out.

19. The fellow that did take in hand
These children for to kill,
Was for a robbery judged to die,
Such was God's blessed will:
Who did confess the very truth,
As here hath been display'd:

The uncle having died in jail,
 Where he for debt was laid.

20. You that executors be made,
 And overseërs eke,
Of children that be fatherless,
 And infants mild and meek,
Take you example by this thing,
 And yield to each his right,
Lest God with suchlike misery
 Your wicked minds requite.

BESSIE BELL AND MARY GRAY

1. O BESSIE BELL and Mary Gray,
 They war twa bonnie lasses;
They biggit a bower on yon burn-brae,
 And theekit it o'er wi' rashes.

2. They theekit it o'er wi' rashes green,
 They theekit it o'er wi' heather;
But the pest cam frae the burrows-town,
 And slew them baith thegither.

3. They thought to lye in Methven kirkyard,
 Amang their noble kin;
But they maun lye in Stronach haugh,
 To biek forenent the sin.

4. And Bessie Bell and Mary Gray,
    They war twa bonnie lasses;
  They biggit a bower on yon burn-brae.
    And theekit it o'er wi' rashes.

GLOSSARY

A

a', all.
aboone, aboon, above.
ae tyne, one harrow-point.
aiblins, perhaps.
aik, oak.
aiken, oaken.
airn, iron.
airt, direction.
aits, oats.
ancyents, ensigns.
Anguish, Angus.
are, plough.
aukeward, back-handed.
ava', of all.

B

ba', ball, football.
bairn, barn, bern, child.
ballup, front, or flap.
bandit, bound.
bassonets, steel skull-caps.
Bateable Land, debateable land, stretch of frontier between the Solway Frith and Scots Dyke.
bedone, adorned.
begane, overlaid.
belive, nimbly, at once, straightway.
ben, further in; to the inner room.
bent, bents, coarse, rough grasses.

berne, fighting-man.
betaken, given, made over.
bette, beat.
bickered, attacked, skirmished.
biek, bask.
bigg, build.
biggit, built.
bigly, commodious, habitable.
Billy Blind, a Brownie, or friendly house-spirit.
birl'd, poured.
blaewort, corn bluebottle.
blan, stopped, stayed.
blin, stint, cease.
blink sae brawlie, glance so bravely.
blint, blinded.
boote, help.
borrow, ransom.
boun, go.
bowne, ready; get ready; made ready, gone.
brae, hillside; river-bank; brow.
brain, mad.
brawn, calf.
breeme, fierce.
breer, brier.
brent, straight, smooth.
brere, brier.
brie, brow.
brittling, cutting up.
brodinge, growing, sprouting.
broken men, outlaws.
brink, brook, enjoy.

busk, array.
busk and boun, trim up and prepare to go.
busked, dressed.
buskit, attired.
buss, bush, clump.
but, ben, in the outer and the inner rooms.
by lane, alone, of itself.
byre, cow-house.

C

camovine, camomile.
cannie, gently.
cante, spirited.
capull-hyde, horse-hide.
care-bed, sick-bed.
carline, old woman.
carp, talk.
cham'er, chamber.
channerin', fretting.
chapp'd, knocked.
chess, jess, strap.
cleed, clothe.
cleiding, clothing.
clifting, cleft.
cloth in grain, scarlet cloth.
cloutie, full of clouts, patched.
Collayne, Cologne steel.
corbies, ravens.
couth, word.
craig, rock.
cramasie, cramoisie, crimson.
cryance, yielding, cowardice.
curch, kerchief, coif.

D

dapperpy, diapered.
deas, dais, pew.

dee, do.
deid, death.
dight, done, doomed; ordained.
dighted, dressed.
dill, dole, grief.
discreeve, discover.
distrain, distress.
doen, betaken.
doo, dove.
dought, could.
dow, n., dove; v., can, are able to.
dowie, adj., dismal, gloomy; doleful; heavy, sorrowful; adv., dolefully.
downa, cannot, have not the force to.
dree, suffer.
drie, endure.
drumly, turbid.
dule ye dree, grief you suffer.
dyke, wall; ditch.

E

eare, ere, ayre, heir
eldritch, unearthly.
eme, uncle.
even cloth, smooth cloth.
examine, put to the test.
ezar, for "mazer," maple?

F

fail, turf.
fankit, entangled.
farley, wondrous strange.
fashes, troubles.
fashion, form, beauty.
fee, wages.

fere, feere, mate, consort.
fend, provide for.
fell, high land, fit only for
pastures.
ferlie, marvel.
fette, fetched.
fettled, prepared.
fey, destined to die.
flatter'd, tossed afloat.
fleed, flood.
fleet, floor.
fley'd, frightened.
flyte, scold.
forbye, aside.
forehammers, sledge-ham-
mers.
fountain-stone, font.
freits, ill omens.
freyke, bold fellow.
frush, brittle.
fule, fowl.
fur', furrow.
fytle, division of a ballad.

G

gang by the hauld, walk by
holding on to the hand.
ganging, going.
gar'd, made.
gar'd her drie, caused her to
suffer.
gare, gore, strip; a seam of a
shirt.
garl, gravel?
gar me to dine, give me my
fill, entertain me (at fight-
ing).
gate, way.
gid, went.
gilt, gold.

gin, trick, or sleight, of the
door-latch.
gleed, live coal.
glent, glanced, darted.
glo', glove.
Glore, Glory.
God's pennye, earnest or
luck-penny.
good loade, heavily.
gore, skirt, waist.
gowans, daisies.
gowany, daisied.
graithed, harnessed,in armor.
grat, cried.
gravat, cravat, collar.
greet, cry.
greeting, wailing, crying.
greves, groves.
growende, ground.
grund-wa', ground-wall.
gryselye, in a grisly manner,
terribly.
gryte, great.
gurly, rough, surly.

H

ha', manor-house.
hae, have.
haik ye up, hold you in sus-
pense.
hale, whole.
hallow seat, holy man's or
hermit's cave.
Hambleton, Hamilton.
hansell, foretaste.
happers, mill-hoppers.
harp and carp, play and recite
(as a minstrel).
haud, hold, keep.
hauld, place of shelter.

hause, neck.
heght, promised.
hele, health.
hnigers, hangings, curtains.
hollins, holly.
hooly, slowly, softly.
houms, water-meads.
hoved, abode.
husbands, husbandmen.

I

ilka, ilkae, each, either.
in fere, in company, together.
in that ilk, in that same (moment), then and there.
I'se, I shall.

J

jawing, surging.
jimp, slim, slender.
jo, sweetheart.
jow, heat, toll.

K

kail, kale, colewort.
kaim, kame, comb.
kell, hair-net.
ken, know.
kep, kepped, catch, caught.
kevels, kevils, lots.
kinnen, rabbits.
kist, chest.
knave-bairn, man-child.
kye, kine, cattle.

L

laigh, low.
laird, a land-holder, with rank less than that of knight.
lamer, amber.
lap, leapt, sprang.
lave, rest.
laverocks, larks.
lawing, reckoning.
lay, law, faith.
lay land, lea, land not under cultivation.
layne, conceal.
leal, true.
lear, lore, learning.
lease, leash, thong; leasing, falsehood.
lee, *n.*, untilled ground, open plain, grass land; *adj.*, calm, pleasant.
leeve, dear, pleasant, lovely.
'leeve, believe.
lemman, sweetheart.
leugh, laughed.
leven, lawn.
Liddel-rack, a ford on the Liddel.
lift, sky.
lig, lie.
lighter, delivered.
limmer, wretch, jade.
linn, stream, pool (especially below a water-fall).
list, inclination, desire for it.
lith, joint.
lither, rascally, vile.
loof, palm.
loot, let.
loup, leap.
louted, bowed.

lowe, flame; hillock.
lucettes, luces, pikes (heraldic).
ly'ed, lived.
lyke-wake, corpse-watching.
lyne, linden.

M

mae, more.
make, mate, lover.
makes, means.
malison, curse.
manoplie, long gauntlet.
marrow, married mate.
marys, maidens.
masteryes, trials of skill.
maun, must.
may, maid.
meikle, much, great.
meinye, company.
mickle may, mighty maid.
ming'd, mentioned, spoke the name of.
mores, moors.
mort, death of the game.
muir, moor.
my warldis make, my one mate in the world.

N

neen, none, not.
neir, never.
neist, neisten, next.
never a dele, never a bit.
nicker, neigh.
niest, next.
nourice, nurse.

O

on a party, apart.
on the splene, in haste.
ony, any.
our lane, we alone.
ousen, owsen, oxen.

P

pall, fine cloth.
pat, did put.
pit, put.
plat, pleated.
play-feres, playfellows.
poin'd, made forfeit.
prickes, marks.
prins, pins.
pu', pull.
puggish, tramp's.
pyght, pitched.

Q

quarry, dead game.
queet, ankle.
quite, free, clear, unpunished.

R

rank, wild, bold, strong.
reachles on, reckless, careless of.
reane, gutter.
reaving, tearing.
rede, n., counsel; v., advise.
rede I can, counsel I know.
reet, root.
reiver, robber.

rekeles, reckless, wild.
rigg, ridge.
rive, tear.
roke, reek, mist.
row, rowe, roll, wrap.
row-footed, rough-footed.
ryal in rowghte, royal in rout, a king amongst men.
rynde, riven, or flayed.

S

sabelline, sable.
sackless, innocent.
sark, shirt.
saugh, willow.
schoote, thrust, sent quickly.
scroggs, stunted, or scraggy, trees.
scug, screen, expiate.
Seely Court, the Happy Court (of the Fairie·).
settle ye by, keep you waiting aside.
shathmont, six inches.
shaws, woods.
sheave, slice.
shee, shoe.
sheen, *n.*, shoes; *adj.*, shining, bright; beautiful.
sheugh, trench.
shope, shaped, made.
shot-window, bow-window, a window opening on a hinge.
shroggs, shrubs.
siccan, such.
sigh clout, a rag for straining.
silver-gris, a fur of silver-gray.
sin, sun.

single livery, private's uniform.
skaith'd, hurt, wronged.
skeely, skilful.
slack, hollow, dell.
slade, hollow.
slode, split.
snae, snow.
soummin', swimming.
sowm, swim.
spauld, shoulder, *épaule.*
speer, spier, ask.
splent, split or overlapping armor.
stear, stir, commotion.
steven, voice.
stey, steep.
stot, steer.
stounde, time.
stown, stolen.
stowre, press of battle.
straik, stroke.
stratlins, stragglings.
striped, thrust.
styrande, stirring, rousing.
stythe, place, station.
swapp'd, swapt, smote.
swat, sweated.
sweaven, dream.
syke, marsh.

T

tae, toe.
taen, taken.
tak', take, catch.
targats, round ornaments.
tett, tuft.
than, then.
theek, thatch.
theekit, thatched.

the **streen,** yestreen, yesterday.
thie, thigh.
thimber, stout.
thoe, those.
thole, suffer, be capable of.
threap, argue.
threescore rood in twinne,
sixty rods apart.
tift, puff, whiff.
tine, lose.
tirled, rattled.
tocherless, without a dowry.
tone, one of two.
toom, empty.
trew, trust.
trysted, invited.
twin, break in two.
twine, twine-cloth, shroud.
twinn'd, robbed, deprived.
twyned, taken away, be-
reaved.
tyde, time of day.
tyne, lose.

U

under night, in the night.
unsett steven, time not ap-
pointed.
until, into, to.

V

vaward, vanguard.
virr, vigor.
voyded, gave room, ran off.

W

wadded, wagered.
wall, well.
wame, womb.
wane, dwelling, arbor; host,
multitude.
wap, wrap.
war', worse.
warldis meed, world's reward, most precious thing
in the world (*or perhaps
corrupted from* warldis
make, mate).
warsle, wrestle.
waryson, reward.
wat, wetted.
water-kelpy, water-sprite.
weal, clench.
weed, clothes.
weel-faur'd may, well-fa-
vored maiden.
weird, doom.
well-wight, strong, lusty;
brave.
wear'd her in, led her into.
wight, sturdy.
wightlye, briskly, stoutly.
wighty, sturdy, active.
win on, continue.
withershins, around against
the sun.
won, win, get; dwell.
wood, crazy, mad, fierce;
wild with delight.
woodwele, woodlark, thrush.
wood-wroth, mad with rage.
wouche, evil.
wroken, avenged.
wud, mad.
wynne, joy.
wyte, blame.

Y

yae, each.
yate, gate.
yeard-fast, fast in earth.

yede, went.
yelpe, brag.
yett, gate.
yode, walked, went.

INDEX OF TITLES AND FIRST LINES

(Titles are set in capitals and small capitals; first lines, in upper and lower case.)

373

JUL   3 '84   T

H54911

PR1181 $29.95
B612   The Best English and Scottish ballads.
1982

Please Do Not Remove Card From Pocket

YOUR LIBRARY CARD

may be used at all library agencies. You
are, of course, responsible for all materials
checked out on it. As a courtesy to others
please return materials promptly. A service
charge is assessed for overdue materials.

The SAINT PAUL PUBLIC LIBRARY

DEMCO